Fearing No Evil

"One woman's life of tragedy and victory"

Autobiography
by
Myrna L. Goehri Etheridge

the Martin Press

Fearing No Evil

The author acknowledges use of the following copyright material:

Finis Jessings Dake, "Dake's Annotated Reference Bible"
© 1979 Dake Bible Sales, Inc.

J. Marcus Haggard, "How the Believer Can Take Control Over His or Her Mind Home Business and Country"
© 1980 Haggard

Frank and Ida Mae Hammond, "Pigs in the Parlor: A Practical Guide to Deliverance"
© 1973 Impact Books, Inc.

Jim Hylton, "Broken Curses and Received Blessings"
Fulness Magazine, Vol. 5, No. 4, July-August, 1982, pp. 20-23

James Strong, "Strong's Exhaustive Concordance"
© 1894 Crusade Bible Publishers, Inc.

Robert Young, "Young's Analytical Concordance"
© Associated Publishers and Authors, Inc.

**LIBRARY OF CONGRESS CATALOGING
IN PUBLICATION DATA**

Etheridge, Myrna L. Goehri
Fearing No Evil

ISBN 0-941018-12-1
Library of Congress Catalog Card No. 84-60229
Printed in the United States of America
10 9 8 7 6 5 4 3

Dedication

My thanks to the ones who lived this book with me and the one who helped me relive it. And to Diane and Dan for their patient readings.

Table of Contents

1

Bumble-Bees and Touch-Me-Nots

The lazy July day descended upon the sleepy college town of Jonesboro, Arkansas. The college houses looked as though they had smiles upon their tiny brick fronts as the rising sun cast split shadows from the east upon their north-facing fronts.

I looked from the bathroom window as I stretched the sleep from my body. The sounds of other college students alerted me of the need for speed in putting the bread into the toaster and the eggs into the pan. "Gary," I called softly, "are you almost ready for breakfast?"

"Oh, I guess so," came from the breathy yawn.

I smiled and laid the breakfast on to the table. We ate without speaking. I often wondered if every couple silently endured each other at breakfast time.

My husband interrupted my thoughts, "I'm through with class at eleven-thirty today. Have lunch on time, please, because I have my first practice today—on my own."

He kissed me goodbye, then went out the door. I watched through the window. He gracefully moved to the far side of the blue 1959 Chevrolet and placed his young, athletic body in the driver's seat.

He really was handsome. I looked at those blond waves of hair and that lean, strong body that caused his path to be filled with admirers. His eyes, close-up, were surrounded with lots of long brown lashes to match the brown eyes. His smile was sunshine. I considered myself lucky.

I looked at the clock on the stove. It was nearly eight, and the boys were making noises in the bedroom. From other houses I could hear a warm and loving symphony of life. There was laughter, television, radio, and children crying. There were pots and pans clanging to answer the calls for breakfast.

As I fixed breakfast for my sons, I was surrounded by the sounds of nature. They were less intense, yet to me the quality was greater. I smiled at God's creations. The sounds of the bumble-bees indicated that they were busily collecting nectar. Because I had studied Biology I knew they pushed the pollen into ingenious little baskets on their legs. Their buzzing was growing steadily louder with each addition to their food stores. They sounded as though they were singing as they collected their winter food on a long row of carefully-tended touch-me-nots. These flowers, peeking from the axils of the leaves, lifted their multitude of pink and red blossoms toward the sky. They knew to seek the warmth and light from the sun. The bumble-bees did not seem to notice that the flowers were not fragrant. They just knew that they had plenteous nectar that they instinctively were to collect. Nor did the bees seem to mind the fine, bristly pubescense which covered the bodies of the erect, sparsely-branched flowering plants. They buzzed, happily dressed in their fine, yellow-striped coats. They were secure in God's love and provision for them. Kirk, almost three and the joy of my life, sat across the table from his brother, Keith and me. As he skillfully ate his eggs with toast and milk, his eyes twinkled as he prepared to say something. What eyes they were! Brown with long lashes, and except for the straight blond hair he was almost a carbon copy of his father. I wondered how he had missed the wavy hair.

"Mom," Kirk said to get my attention.

"Yes, Dearie," I replied, now at attention.

"If I eat everything and wash my hands, will I be able to go out and play?" Kirk asked.

"Actually, you have almost finished. Let me see. You have finished the cereal and ice cream. The orange juice is gone. Your eggs and toast have almost disappeared. All you haven't eaten are your expectorate and antibiotics. You did take the enzymes with the cereal, didn't you?" I asked, checking carefully for the intake of medication we heavily depended upon.

"Yes, I did!" he answered joyfully.

"Keith, watch it! That was my finger you bit," I quickly retorted to my three-month-old-son.

Actually, Keith had a right to bite me. I had almost forgotten that I was feeding him. Talking to Kirk, I neglected to feed him a few bites of his breakfast, and the child in my lap was just reminding me of his need. I hugged him to me and continued feeding him as Kirk and I finished our conversation.

"I washed my hands. Mom, I want to go out and play!" Kirk reported.

"Are you going to play with Autumn?" I inquired.

"No, I'll just play alone," he replied with the same twinkle as before.

"All right, you may. You have been a very good boy to eat your breakfast so well and wash your hands. But, please tell me if you go out of our yard. Will you?" I asked, expecting him to obey explicitly any directions he was given.

"O.K.," he replied simply as he walked to the door.

He made a pit-pat sound in his tennis shoes as he walked across a concrete carport. The little walkway was shaded this time of the day. The carport was deserted. The carport was his own private raceway.

Today the hum of the bees was attracting Kirk. Many times he had wandered to the row of flowers and watched the bumble-bees do their work. He was entranced by God's chorus of working, flying wonders. His eyes shone brightly, and his warm friendship for the bees was reflected in his smile.

Often he let the lone bee park its fat body on the back of his hand. He would peer closely at the striped bee. Sometimes he even talked gently to his friend. He thought, bees never caught colds. They did not come down with the flu. They did not take playthings or mess them up. You could depend on the bumble-bees to be there in the morning, ready to play. He smiled. His hand stretched out to get closer to one of the adored bees.

"Ouch, touch-me-nots sure are sticky!" he muttered as he touched one of the flowers with a bee on it. "No, I'm not going to hurt you," he said softly to the bee. "Bumbl-ee-bee, come here!" He was innocently pleased as the bee sat down. Two of God's creatures looked at each other.

The bumble-bee walked about in the palm of the small hand. As it walked, the boy began to squirm just the least little bit. The walking was a new feeling. Usually the bee would light on the back of his hand, not the palm. It tickled.

"Hey, bumbl-ee-bee, that tickles," he said to the bee as he slightly closed his hand.

The bee became alarmed by the movement of the hand and responded. The frightened bee stung the boy.

Kirk was grief-struck. The pain in his hand was bad, but the pain in his heart was worse. His friend the bumble-bee hurt him. Could he not depend on the bumble-bees either?

"Mom! Mommie!!" he half cried as he ran around the edge of the house. The door was ajar about a foot. He popped through the doorway and into the kitchen where I had turned to meet him.

"Kirk, what is wrong?" I demanded loudly! This kind of entrance was most unusual, and I knew it.

He held out the already swelling hand. The palm of his right hand was beginning to puff up. As he extended the hand he said with sadness, the start of tears and disappointment, "The bumbl-ee-bee never bited me before!"

I was aghast. "You were playing with the bumble-bees?" I said in disbelief, realizing for the first time the origin of the swelling.

He nodded his head. The tears welled up in his eyes.

"Well, I'm sure the bee didn't know that you wouldn't hurt it. All a bee knows how to do when it is afraid is to sting you," I said as I took him up into my arms and carried my disappointed child toward the kitchen sink.

I put some ice on the hand. Then I hugged my son as I considered what to do next. "God, help," I prayed silently.

I looked at the hand. The little palm had swollen so the thumb section of the hand was puffed up and painted with a tiny red mark. Surely I did not need to call the doctor. Kirk wasn't alergic to bee stings. Tears came to my eyes too. I realized how important Kirk's friendship with the bees was. When a child has cystic fibrosis he can not always play with other children. The bees were his dear, faithful friends. They didn't have infections like the children did. I sniffed too. When I looked at Kirk I realized that the bee's defenses were affecting him emotionally worse than physically. Finally, I remembered Uncle Herbie's remedy for a yellow jacket sting my sister had long ago. I said,

"Let's go see Mr. Jake and see if he has some chewing tobacco we can use to put on the sting."

"Mr. Jake's at school, but Margaret is home 'cause the door is open," Kirk helped.

I took Keith out of the jump chair and realized he had been looking at us with fear during the ordeal. I hugged him and took Kirk's well hand in mine as we hurried through the kitchen door. We walked quickly across the lawn onto the carport of the next house east of ours.

"Margaret, are you home?" I called to my neighbor.

"Yes, I'm making the bed. Come on in." came the friendly reply from within.

We entered.

"How are you?" Margaret inquired.

"We have a problem. It seems that Kirk's friendship with the bumble-bees has a kink in it," I said simply as the swelling hand was offered for inspection.

"Oh, dear me! Does it hurt, Kirk?" Margaret inquired in her sweet, gentle voice.

"The bumbl-ee-bee never bited me before," he responded as before. He did not seem to note any physical pain.

Margaret peered at the tiny red mark in the swollen heel of Kirk's hand and asked, "Do you think some tobacco would do something to help draw the poison out of the sting?" She was perceptive.

Kirk nodded his head.

Margaret went to the tobacco jar and realized the next problem. Jake wasn't home.

"Goodness, who will chew the tobacco?" Margaret said aloud.

We looked at each other and began to giggle.

Both the boys watched intently as the adults acted like children. They had no idea that chewing tobacco would be so funny. They did not realize how offensive the simple task of chewing tobacco could be to the two women.

Margaret and I began mixing some of the tobacco with a little water. That did not work very well. We enjoyed trying to use our creativity to make the tobacco gooey. We finally mixed the tobacco without chewing it. Neither of us could bring ourselves to do that.

Margaret took the swollen hand and gently applied the moist, gooey tobacco to the tender sting. Kirk began to relax, and it showed in his face.

"Momma, it feels better," he stated as he smiled lovingly at Margaret.

Keith was nestled in my arms as I sat still, resting on one of the kitchen chairs. Kirk walked to the sturdy oak table where I was seated.

"Thank you, Margaret, you are a dear." I gathered the boys for leaving. "Gary will be home from classes shortly, and Keith needs to be fed and changed, so I must hurry."

Kirk had gone to the front of the house. Keith and I went into the house since he needed to be changed. Though I loved this tiny child, I cringed each time I saw the skeletal markings through the skin of his emaciated body. His stools were the usual frothy, yellow, malodorous consistency.

We ignored these problems and loved each other with typical baby-mother talk. I prayed, "God grant us the grace to accept your will."

The pleasant lunch was shared in a warm, considerate way and following the sharing was nap time for the boys. Sometimes I rested with them, but today I had decided to sit in the lounge chair in the yard and read from the Bible. The Bible fell open to my favorite, Psalm 23. I began to read,

> "The Lord is my shepherd: I shall not want. He maketh me to lie down in green pastures; He leadeth me beside the still waters. He restoreth my soul; He leadeth me in the paths of righteousness for His name's sake. Yea, though I walk through the valley of the shadow of death, I will fear no evil; for thou art with me; thy rod and thy staff they comfort me."

I stopped reading and looked through my tears toward the row of carefully-tended houses within which some of the faculty lived. I prayed earnestly within my heart. "Lord, I know you are my shepherd. I get next to the edge of the cliff at times and you take care of me. But Lord, help my babies. They are so sick. I can't even talk about it without crying. Poor little Keith probably will not even live through the winter. Help me to accept that, if I have to. I don't want to. Please work a miracle, if it is Your will and Your plan. If not, help me to be strong. Help me not to fear. Help me to live each day to its fullest. Oh, God, I know You made this world and the beauty I see. Help me to find only good in each day. Please, Lord, help me walk through the valley. I can't go without You. I'm too afraid." I was sobbing.

Gary's arrival interrupted my thoughts, "We got a letter from Mom and Dad today. They are going to come for a visit the second week in August, so we can go for a short vacation."

"You mean just you and me?" I said in amazement.

"Yes, Honey. Just us. Where do you want to go?" Gary asked.

"We don't have any money. Where can we go?" I asked without hope.

"They thought of that. They are babysitting and making sure we go," he comforted.

"Great! Your parents are really wonderful. You decide where we will go. I'll go along for the ride."

"O.K. We are going to Nashville. I'd like to visit the Hermitage and the replica of the Parthenon. The time I visited the capitol building the tour guide said it was unique, but just now I don't remember how. There are a bunch of good Civil War museums there too. We'll enjoy being there together."

2

Happy Birthday To Me

"Zoom, zoom, zoo-oo-mm," came the engine noises from the driveway raceway.

Kirk was pedaling vigorously around the figure-eight raceway on the carport. The August sun warmed the air.

Breakfast had been about an hour ago. He still felt the energy he had gained from sleeping in the mist tent. He no longer considered the sounds of ice being replenished during the night as anything unusual. He only vaguely recalled coughing during the night. He had lived nearly three years with these sounds. He could not recall that they began during his eighth month. Since then he had slept constantly in the mist tent. The hum of the air compressor and ice replacement had been his usual night music since then.

His Buster Brown tennis shoes were circling as though he were an olympic rider, but, in a short while the burst of energy was past. He was thinking about a banana. His favorite snack was a banana. The digestive enzymes were easier to swallow with it than with plain milk. At least, he believed they were.

The race car tricycle was parked, and the driver darted into the kitchen. His chest expanded. As it did, the exertion showed his prominent breast bone. It was curved noticeably outward due to the stress with which his heart and lungs contended daily.

"Mom, I want a banana. O.K.?"

I heard him move toward the fruit. He knew they would be on the counter top. I continued putting on makeup as I called to him, "Remember to take one of the enzymes."

He put the enzyme pill on the end of the banana. It looked like a tiny crown. He took aim and bit around it. The enzyme pill went into his stomach with the first bite.

I was washing the cleanser off my face. Kirk was watching me. I grinned at Kirk as he watched. He ate so many bananas that I sometimes found myself wondering if he would turn into a monkey. He did do a lot of funny things. Maybe he was part monkey? He continued to watch. I didn't mind.

Keith was in the second generation hand-me-down jump chair. He watched Kirk walk into the small bathroom. Keith smiled his four-toothed grin. He was brown-eyed and blond-haired as his older brother. His gaunt face showed the contentment of a happy four-month-old. He is happy, I thought. He was also ill. At four months he weighed ten pounds. He was twenty-nine inches tall. He had the same inborn, chemically malfunctioning body as Kirk. He bounced with joy in the many-times-redone canvas jump seat. His toys were plastic spoons and often-chewed-and-washed beads. He had begun sitting up well enough to enjoy the chair.

We knew togetherness in the bathroom, not only because the room was small, but because the feelings of love were visible. Each of us was vital to the other. The boys sensed that they were special to their father and me. I realized that they were unique and real treasures to me. Soon, I feared, they would be gone from me. Each minute with them was precious to me. The joy of the moment made me smile.

Kirk was looking straight into my face. "When is my birthday?" he asked and he looked at a lipstick he had picked up.

"Tomorrow. Remember, Daddy told you this morning at breakfast—one more day until you are three years old!"

"How old is three?" he queried.

"That is two years older than Keith. But it is not nearly so old as your daddy. He'll be twenty-five years old his next birthday." I held up three fingers.

Kirk mimmicked me. He was holding up three fingers and saying, "Three years old, I be three years old tomorrow!"

I wondered, would he be able to hold up four fingers, or five? Would Keith ever be one? They understood that they had a disease, but thought little of it. We simply talked about other things.

My mind wandered. I knew a bit about biology. Cystic fibrosis was a more gruesome thing to me than if my sons had the plague. With the plague one either recovered or died. With cystic fibrosis the daily possibility of death lingered. What unfortunate luck! Gary and I both inherited the genetic trait for cystic fibrosis. One in twenty, the doctor had said, has this genetic trait. So, one in four-hundred caucasian couples would have the same genetic potential for cystic fibrosis children. How horrible, I thought. I looked at my two wonderful, sick children. I pushed the fears from my mind. I prayed silently, "Be merciful. Grant us a good day," and quickly put on the last part of my makeup.

"Let's go, boys! It's time to exercise with Jack on television," I said as I moved the jump chair to the living room.

Kirk always laughed more than he exercised with the television show. I made faces at him as I exercised. We laughed and enjoyed the thirty minutes. Keith exercised, too, in the jump chair.

When exercise time was over Keith and the jump chair were moved to the kitchen table. That way Keith was able to be talked to at eye level. Kirk placed his favorite record carefully on the stereo. He knew exactly how to operate it. It seemed like the thousandth time to me. Kirk loved it. He sang along as the sing-songy children's poems from Mother Goose were re-enjoyed. I sang the songs to Keith. He crowed.

"Peace porridge ho-ot," sang Kirk.

He soon smelled his favorite porridge. Odors of chicken soup, homemade with lots of carrots, celery and rice floated back to him. Lunch ws almost ready.

Our blue, 1959 model Chevrolet was pulling into the driveway.

I watched as Kirk abruptly stopped the record. He jumped off the cedar chest, now used as a stereo table, and hid behind the door.

Gary's voice was saying warmly as he entered, "Where is Kirk?" pause—then, "Where is my big man?"

The hiding game was played almost daily, always with delightful suspense.

Keith jumped excitedly in the deftly located chair and muttered, "Da, Da." He wanted in on the game, though he was only four months old.

Kirk crouched behind the door. He covered his mouth to keep the laughter and excitement in.

Our togetherness and love showed again as, "There you are!" and a hearty hug fused the look-alikes together.

I retrieved Keith and the chair from the table. I kissed my husband a smack. Gary picked up Keith. That was preliminary to taking Keith to the high chair. I prepared the table for serving lunch.

Thursday, August 16, 1962 Kirk was three years old.

At seven in the morning we were asleep in our small house. One could not say all was quiet because the air compressor was noisily puffing. Air passed through the tubes over the water jar to put water vapor into the mist tent. Keith needed some of the vapor produced. The side flap of the plastic tent was extended to the baby bed where Keith was resting.

The seven-fifteen alarm set us in motion. Soon I was dressed and preparing breakfast. It was usual for me to be up and dressed before Gary got out of bed. This morning I went to the auto. From it I removed a modest-sized fish bowl and two fast-swimming goldfish. There was fish food and a small dip net beside the bowl. I hurried back inside. The fish and equipment were arranged beside Kirk's plate. I smiled as I laid the birthday card with the big three on it in the plate.

I continued the breakfast prepartion as I cajoled, "You boys better hurry up, or it will be noon time."

"Happy birthday to me," sang Kirk. His singing was passable for a three-year-old. He had a funny, squeaky quality to his voice on the "to me" part. That squeaky sound caused Gary and me to laugh aloud.

"Kirk," Gary said as he stopped shaving momentarily, "you are right. Today is the right time to sing to yourself."

I supposed that the comment was put forth because Kirk had been singing to himself for several months. I laughed at the remembrance.

Soon the fish were discovered and a pajama muffled dance was carried out beside the kitchen table. The fish were loved.

Within an hour breakfast was over. Gary was gone to see the coach about something or the other. Keith was bathed and fed. I was getting my makeup on. I wondered what Kirk was up to?

My make-up was finished, so I walked back to the living room and the fish bowl. I gasped when I saw the amount of breakfast my son had lovingly bestowed on the fish.

"Kirk, fish are not used to eating so much food. We will have to take out some of it or they will eat so much food that they will die," I warned.

Together we took out most of the food that Kirk had so generously placed into the fish tank.

"Do not feed the fish any more today. They have had enough food." I said, looking eye-to-eye with my son.

"But Mom, I get hungry for food lots of times a day. George and Harry will starve if I don't feed them when I get hungry." Kirk reasoned from his experience.

"If you feed the fish as many times a day as you eat, they *will* die. That's right! You must not feed them that much! Fish don't need as much food as you do." I pleaded.

The next day the little fisherman was again overfeeding Harry and George.

Monday morning Kirk alerted the world, "Mom, Dad!, Come quick! George is on top of the water!"

Both of us came quickly.

"Son, did you feed the fish like your mom told you?" Gary asked.

"No. I fed them whenever I ate. So they wouldn't get hungry," he stated honestly.

"Kirk, George is dead. We'll have to bury him," Gary stated. He added, "If you feed Harry that much, he may not live either."

Kirk looked very sad, as though he might cry. "How do you bury anything?" asked the practical child.

"We'll get your little shovel and dig a small hole in the ground and put George into it," Gary guided.

I watched as they solemnly dipped George out of the fish bowl with the net and took him for a last trip out of the house. George was gently placed into the ground. Kirk and Gary held hands beside the flowers while Gary said a prayer.

"Jesus, take care of George for Kirk. Thank you." he prayed comfortingly.

The next day the little fisherman was overfeeding Harry.

I walked into the living room as the final, "There, Harry, now you will feel good!" reached my ears.

Kirk, you know that you are not to feed Harry so much. Just a pinch is enough," I scolded dramatically.

"But Mom, I just feed him when I get hungry!" Kirk defended.

"Obviously, that was too much for George!" I stated unkindly.

"Oh, Mom, I miss George!"

With this Kirk began to cry. I went to him. Kneeling on the floor, I embraced him. I held my sobbing son to my breast. I kissed his forehead.

"I'm sure you do. He was awfully nice," I agreed.

As I held Kirk to let him rid himself of grief, I again became aware of the special sweet odor of his perspiration. Keith had the same odor when he perspired. My lips had kissed his forehead. The taste of the salty kiss warned me that I might some day have occasion to say the same thing of my son. I rocked him gently, as I, too, began to sob. The long months of fighting for my sons' health were wearing on my nerves and body. Most nights were like last night. Keith had begun to choke on phlegm about two in the morning. I was wakened and ran to him. By the time I had dragged the phlegm from his throat, he was nearly blue from lack of oxygen. Then, while he was blue and weak, his stomach had emptied itself. I had bathed him and fed him again after he had gotten back to normal. I wasn't certain how much more of this I could take. These realizations were the basis of my sympathetic sobbing. I rocked us until our tears flowed away. Silently I prayed as I continued rocking. "Father, give me strength and continued patience." My prayer laid my weaknesses before the only source of my strength.

"Squeak!" called Keith from the baby bed.

"Oh, dear, Keith is all by himself," I recalled, drying my eye with one finger.

Kirk popped from my arms, "I'll get a toy for you Keif," he called, running to his brother.

Keith crowed with his usual joy.

Smiling, I got myself set to face my sons. Those two have loved each other like that since we brought Keith home from the hospital. I continued smiling as I remembered waking from a nap when Keith was one week old. I had heard, "That's all right Keif, I'll get your bottle!" Kirk had, too. It was cold, and direct from the refrigerator. At least, I thought, I have been privileged to have the joy of giving birth. Some of the memories that I have are most precious. I went to the boy's room to join the fun.

3

Furnace Off, Flu Shots In

Time had passed quickly since my work had begun as a teacher of music and art. Kirk and I spent many happy afternoons in the libraries of the college and city. He loved books and entertained himself with selecting one or two books while I searched for the resources I needed to teach Art I. With each type of art media came a new collection of books to read and notes to prepare. Visual arts were a hobby for me since I was a child designing my doll's dresses. Now it was helping me to earn our living. Gary approved the job adventure and was an enthusiastic partner. He was as excited about the lift the new adventure was giving me as I was. It was good to feel caught up in the new knowledge. My mind had an outlet for the creative spirit within me. My days seemed more like hours or minutes than days. My spirit was vibrant. The years since Kirk was diagnosed as cystic fibrosis had been strained, yet basically happy. Being a stubborn creature, I had decided to value my child by the day never allowing thoughts about when he was grown. That would take care of itself when the time came, I reasoned. He was three years and two months old now, and so far my theory had worked. Now with the challenge of my work I gathered strength each day. My nights were short. Always they were interrupted by coughing spells and calls for care or help by my sons. Though I was anemic again, I was mentally content. Often I read from the Bible as I fed Keith in the morning. He listened attentively most of the time, eventhough he didn't understand much. How much could a six-month old child understand? I wondered as I read from St. Mathew 6:25-34. Keith listened as he finished his bottle.

> "...Take no thought for your life, what ye shall eat, or what ye shall drink; nor yet for your body, what ye shall put on. Is not the life more than meat, and the body than raimant? (26) Behold the fowls of the air; for they sow not, neither do they reap, nor gather into barns; yet your heavenly Father feedeth them. Are ye not much better than they? (27) Which of you by taking thought can add one cubit unto his stature? (28) And why take ye thought for raiment? Consider the lilies of the field, how they grow; they toil not, that even Solomon in all his glory was not arrayed like one of these."

Keith belched loudly.

"You are excused! Really, son, I was reading God's Word!" I shamed.

"A goo," said Keith.

"Yes, you better say you are sorry," I said and continued reading silently until I got to verse thirty-three.

"But seek ye first the kingdom of God, and His righteousness; and all these things shall be added to you"

"Father," I prayed softly, "I've sought you since I first believed as a nine-year-old. You are great and powerful. Please find it in your will to heal my sons. Please, I beg you, consider your daughter. Give me what I need—just need."

Maggie, our babysitter, stepped to the door, "Morning," she called.

Things went on smootly until one night in the middle of the night. The house was dark. Kirk got up from his bed shivering in the darkness. He knew that we would warm him. He quickly entered the master bedroom where we were sleeping.

"Mom, Momma! Wake up!" Kirk insisted.

Vaguely from the depths of my subconscious level of sleep I woke to the verbal prodding.

"Um-hum," I mumbled, "What do you want?"

"I'm cold, let me sleep with you!" Kirk pleaded.

"Cold? How cold?" I wakened and began to get alarmed. Why was it cold? It shouldn't be. What about Keith? I thought as I said, "Get under the covers and warm up."I hugged Kirk. He was shivering with cold.

"Gary, wake up. The furnace must be off. It's cold in the house. I'm going to get Keith," I said bounding from the bed.

I nearly ran to Keith. Keith was crying softly.

"Keith, Momma is sorry! Bet baby is cold, too," I said holding the cold, shivering child to my body to warm him.

His body shook trying to warm him. He was very wet and cold. I thought how the combination of these might affect him. I shivered too. Grabbing a dry sleeper and diaper I hurried and took him into the warm master bed. I could change him later under the covers.

Gary was struggling at lighting the furnace. The cover was removed from the front and a loud "ouch!" came from getting a scorched finger.

He returned saying, "I don't understand why the furnace went off. The men from the shop checked it this week."

"They were here, weren't they?"

"Maggie said they were. Here, let me help warm the boys."

Gary got into bed carefully beside Kirk.

"Come here big man. Get close to Daddy so we can warm up. How is Keith?" Gary querried.

"He's warmer than before, but I'm going to get a bottle of milk and warm it. I'd better give more antibiotics just in case"—I stopped short of verbalizing my fear.

I was quickly out of bed and into my housecoat. I prepared the bottle and antibiotics and went back to bed as soon as possible. It was still cold.

Giving the bottle to Keith, I shed my housecoat, entered the family bed and asked, "How cold was it supposed to get tonight?"

Gary mumbled, "Freezing at least."

"I'm glad it isn't colder!" I said as I gave the measured amount of antibiotic to each son.

By three-thirty the house had warmed enough for Gary to know it was possible for the boys to get back into their beds.

I took the boys back into their tiny warm room. Kirk crawled under the covers unassisted. Keith was put into the bed surrounded by the warm covers and covered by another. I kissed and patted each son gently, then returned exhausted to our bedroom.

Six-thirty came very early. I closed the door of the boys' room quietly and we began preparing for our day of activities in a subdued way.

"Gary, be sure you check the temperature charts at lunch. If either of the boys shows a rise or drop in temperature have Maggie give a teaspoon of Acromyacin every three hours starting at lunch. When Maggie gets here I'll tell her to give it when the boys have breakfast." I was worried so Gary overlooked my telling him in such detail what he already knew.

He nodded, sleepily.

Keith began crying. I went to him quickly and took him to the kitchen where breakfast had warmed the air more than in his room.

"It's bath time for Keife, baby!" I said imitating Kirk's way of saying Keith without the "th" sound. Keith smacked. He liked baths, but he was hungry. Soon he was splashing as usual enjoying the morning ritual.

I smacked back and said, "Are you hungry? Momma will feed you as soon as you get all cleaned up and smelling sweet again."

Keith smacked, crowed and splashed the water with his hands.

"Well, looks like the cold night did not spoil your usual good nature. Hope Kirk is the same." I said relieved of the strain of worry.

Keith cooperated by getting clothes on for the day as quickly as possible. He knew that this had to be done before he would be fed. I kept the routine exactly the same so the boys would know what to expect and feel secure. It was enough that they were genetically ill. The least I could do, I thought was to be certain they were well-adjusted, secure children. They were strictly disciplined and loved devotedly. As the Doctor in St. Louis Children's Hospital warned and guided, we were living. We had taken care of them like we did not think they would live until tomorrow and disciplined them like we thought they would live to be one-hundred.

The instant the last shoe was tied Keith began smacking.

I laughed, "That's right, it's breakfast time!" Keith hung on as I carried him on my left hip as I prepared an egg and toast for him. The cereal was mixed with the milk and enzymes. Keith was fed a bit of cereal every few steps to keep him happy. He smacked when he needed a bite.

In the high chair he enjoyed the eggs and toast. I fed him the poached egg. Keith held his own toast and took a bite when it suited him. He was learning to drink juice from a cup with the enclosed top and spout on it.

The last part of breakfast for Keith was a bottle of milk and getting his temperature taken. The bottle was fun. If he were not being held and snuggled he would have strongly objected to the temperature part. He grimaced when I put that thermometer under his arm and held it down for three minutes. Three minutes was a short time for an adult, but to a six-month-old boy it was nearly too long. He squirmed.

The temperatures remained normal for both the boys. We thanked God for that.

"Good morning, Donnie. This is Myrna. Have we had any sick youngins at Central Baptist Church this week?" I asked.

"Good morning to you! Everyone was well as of Wednesday night. Are you going to be with us today for worship?"

"The boys are well and with the news you just gave me, I think I can say we will see you in Sunday School."

"Good! I was concerned that the cool weather might keep you from being able to be at church," Donnie commented understanding the situation.

As I hung up the phone I sang to the household as an alarm clock. "Everybody ought to go to Sunday School, Sunday School, Sunday School, The men and the women, and the boys and the girls, Everybody ought to go to Sunday School." I paused, then commented, "Kirk is the first bath boy today. Come on sleepy head, we are going to go to Sunday School. All the kids are well!" I was changing Keith's diaper as I talked to Kirk.

"Oh, Goodie!" Definitely excited and thinking, Kirk asked, "What should I wear?"

"Please wear your navy blue corduroy pants and your white shirt and tie with your nylon coat," I said specifically. He was capable of remembering lengthy directions. I knew because I tested his ability often. I smiled as I heard him ask directions for something I had forgotten.

"Can I wear my new shoes and blue socks?"

"Yes, you may wear them. Come on, it's bath time for you!" I encouraged, helping gather the clothes he was to wear.

Gary heard the preparations and knew he must be up soon. He helped feed everyone breakfast on Sunday mornings. He also completed preparing the lesson he taught to a class of high school boys.

Kirk and I sang several other Sunday School songs as I bathed him in the kitchen sink. We both laughed about the situation of his size compared to the size of the sink. This had become usual. The elephant in the kiddie pool was what I called him.

Keith heard us singing. He was busy batting one of the butterflies of the mobile on his bed while he waited. He smacked, thinking about food. The butterflies and singing made him happy too. He voiced his joy. He crowed loudly and ended with, "Da Da."

"Somebody calling me?" Gary answered merrily.

Keith crowed again.

We continued preparing for going to church. Kirk was completely dressed and was playing with a small rubber ball. It went under the couch. He retrieved it and continued playing.

Keith had been through his morning ritual and was playing and jumping contently in his jump chair in the living room.

Kirk began teasing him. "Want my ball, Keif?"

Just when Keith would reach, Kirk would withdraw the ball. Two times of this and Keith let out a loud "Squeak!"

"Sush, Keif!" Kirk commanded.

"Kirk, stop that," Gary corrected.

Presently another "Squeak!" came from Keith.

I walked from the bedroom where I was dressing to reinforce Gary's direction from the bathroom.

"Kirk, stop that!" I paused. Kirk had dust all over the knees of his Sunday pants. "Look at you! How did you get dust all over the front of your pants?" I scolded and asked angrily.

"My ball went under the couch, so I went to bring it out," Kirk defended.

"You go to the couch and sit down. You are not to be on the floor anymore!" I sternly commanded as I brushed the dust from his pants.

Kirk sat down. He was upset and angry, too. He dared not disobey me because I seldom got so upset as this with him. There was a strained silence. Gary reinforced my anger by simply saying Kirk should be ashamed. Kirk was.

At church the boys were taken to the two sections of the nursery department. Keith was in the birth through one-year-of-age department. Kirk was in the three-year-old section of the next department.

"Hello Kirk!" said Mrs. Maggie Gregson kindly. "We've been looking for you. Jennifer has been expecting you."

These two youngsters had been friends, and when they saw each other they ran together and hugged each other. Gregson and I smiled at each other.

As soon as the boys were settled I left for my own class.

Gregson summoned the children by saying, "Children, we are going to play a game. Let's all sit in front of me on the floor."

Kirk went up to her and said, "Hold me, please."

She did, expecting he was needing some sort of special attention.

The activities went on. The children sang action songs and talked about how Jesus loved them.

"Kirk, you can get down now. It's time to play with the other children," the loving woman said.

Kirk replied, "No, I can't!"

"Why not?" she finally asked.

"I got all dusty this morning and my momma told me NOT to get on the floor anymore!" Kirk said emphatically.

The nursery ladies smiled at the strangeness of the situation. They marveled at the obedience of this child they had learned to love and admire. They decided to hold Kirk so he would be in the group. Without forcing him he could play and obey his mother at the same time. They wondered at my command. Keith slept next door to Kirk (on his stomach as usual) with the "Wanted Wet or Dry" showing. The nursery helper patted him gently as a tear trickled down her cheek. She knew how thin and ill this child was. She also knew how much we loved him.

The parents came at eleven-thirty to pick up their children from the nurseries. Some children cried, just to let their parents know they were missed, as the parents arrived. Seldom was a child really unhappy in this well-staffed and equipped nursery.

Keith was still asleep. When Kirk came into the "Baby Nursery" as he called it I was asked to come over to Mrs. Gregson. I was puzzled.

"Myrna, we had to hold Kirk all morning," Mrs. Gregson stated.

"All two and one-half hours?" I asked in amazement.

Mrs. Gregson nodded yes.

"Why?" I asked not understanding what had happened.

"It seems you told Kirk not to get on the floor anymore! So—he wouldn't," she explained.

My face began to flush. "Oh, I didn't mean at church! I'm terribly embarrassed, please forgive me," I asked in my remorse for my anger at Kirk.

"Of course," she said gently, "I wish my kids would obey me that well."

"I'll explain to Kirk on the way home so that he will not react like this again," I assured, "Thank you for being so sweet about this."

We greeted friends as we made our way to the parking lot and our auto. We loved church. We felt new energy because of encouragement from our fellow believers. Our own worship of God gave us strength to face the harsh realities of our lives.

The conversation in our car on the way home was dust-oriented.

"But you told me not to get on the floor anymore" Kirk reminded me, "So, I didn't."

My head wobbled. I didn't know if I should nod yes or no! He was an obedient child. My training beginning at six-months had worked well! I thought of the often-repotted plant that was the test of his will against mine. The swollen hand and weakened plant had set a pattern of obedience that was sure, as his actions showed today. Gary smiled. He must be remembering too.

My thoughts went to the subject at hand. I asked, "Remember, I want you to play with the kids at church. I don't care if you get dusty at church. I just want you to be clean when you get there. Mrs. Gregson doesn't have enough arms to hold all the boys and girls. Do you understand?"

"I guess so," Kirk said near tears. "I need some lovin'!"

He walked sideways toward me in the car seat.

"Me too!" I said softly to my son who was now close to me. "Come here," I said as I motioned for Kirk to sit on one-half on my lap. Keith was scooted over to make room.

"Wet or dry—dusty or not, we love you," stated Gary sensing our sensitive reactions to the situation.

I kissed Kirk on the nose.

After Sunday dinner, before time for the boys' naps Gary suggested taking some pictures. The temperature had warmed considerably and no coats were required when we were out-of-doors.

Gary had placed a quilt on the back of the auto trunk for the boys to sit on while we took a couple of pictures.

Kirk said,"Kief, hold still or we'll break the camera," as they sat ready for the picture to be taken. This was his grandfather Dude's favorite saying to him. After three or four other poses Keith was placed into Kirk's wagon. Keith was tired. He sat straight and looked at Kirk in fear and submission. Kirk took a haughty pose and said, "Hush, Keif!" Their relationship was recorded in the picture.

On Wednesday afternoon Doctor Kemp had directed his nurse to call us to come to his office for a flu shot on Friday. Maggie relayed the message to me. I returned the call.

"Doctor Kemp's office," Ruth, his nurse answered.

"This is Myrna. The doctor said we were to come in Friday at four o' clock. It may be four-twenty when I get there because of the school traffic. If that is all right I will see you then," I qualified.

"Yes, I'll mark the time. Thank you for calling, Myrna," she concluded.

"We're set, Maggie," I said placing the telephone back onto its cradle. "Will you have the boys ready for me to take to the doctor as soon as I get in from school?"

"Surely, I will," Maggie responded understanding the day and the doctor's appointment.

Friday afternoon both boys assisted Maggie in being ready for the trip to the doctor's office. They greeted me at the door. There was no mention of shots on the way to the doctor's office. Keith deftly sat beside me on the front seat. Kirk sat beside Keith assisting in his care.

Kirk was busy telling Keith how nice Doctor Kemp was and about the small gift he usually got. When we arrived we had a short wait. I was grateful for the few minutes to rest. I sighed. Keith was sitting quietly in my lap. We were enjoying his being held.

Ruth, the nurse, was pleasant and helpful. She never got irritated by Kirk's questions. He asked her about the typewriter. He had never examined an electric one before.

"That is a smart typewriter, Mom, it knows where to go back to when you push that big button!" Kirk told me excitedly as he returned with a book.

"That's interesting," I replied courteously.

"Mom, read to us," Kirk asked.

I began the first sentence when Doctor Kemp said, "Kirk, come in here. How are you? We are going to see how tall you are and how much you weigh."

Sneaky! I thought.

"I'll wait here. You can call me if you want me," I said to Kirk.

"Mom," he pleaded, "come on now."

He had just gotten to the door.

"You chicken!" I said softly. Inside I knew I was more of a coward than he was.

"Kirk, you weigh thirty-six pounds and are thirty-six inches tall." Doctor Kemp sat Kirk on the table in the examining room as he spoke.

At Kirk's back Ruth prepared the flu vaccine.

"We are going to put the medicine in you so you do not get flu this winter," Doctor Kemp continued, "Look at your mother Kirk."

Kirk obeyed. His arm was taken and quickly and deftly the vaccine was administered.

Kirk responded as usual with a loud, "Ahh!" and began to cry.

"It's finished now. We want you to stay well," the doctor assured him as he comforted his patient. He patted Kirk as he lowered him to the floor.

"Keith has to be weighed and measured too," I stated.

"That hurt!" Kirk assured me through tears.

"If you stay well, the little hurt is worth it," I said remembering the pneumonia he had at fourteen months.

Ruth motioned to Kirk, "Come with me, Kirk. I have a surprise for you because you were such a good boy."

Kirk smiled and eagerly followed her into the outer office.

At six and a half months Keith weighed thirteen pounds. He was twenty-nine and a half inches tall. The only place there was enough flesh to give the shot was in the front of the upper leg. I cringed. Keith was looking straight into my face wide-eyed and questioningly. When he cried I fought to hold back my own tears. He was pitiful.

"Mom, nurse gave me a sucker!" Kirk announced to me as I returned to the reception room.

"You were a brave boy. I'm proud of you!" I praised him honestly.

Saturday morning both the boys had low grade fevers when I took their temperatures. I called the Doctor to report.

"Myrna, don't be alarmed. Many children react to a flu shot," the Doctor consoled.

"Should I increase antibiotics?" I inquired.

"No, keep them quiet, warm and give lots of liquids. They should be over the reactions by tomorrow." he replied.

"Thanks, doctor. I'll keep you posted if there are any other changes," I said then returned the receiver slowly to the cradle.

Sunday the boys were better. Donnie informed me that a group of six-year-olds had chicken pox. The boys and I stayed home from church. We definitely didn't need another virus.

Since I was at home in the mood to cook with all the school work done and the house cleaned, I fixed beef roast and baked a cake for our lunch.

The food was ready as Gary drove into the driveway. We enjoyed the pot roast, mashed potatoes, slaw and cake.

Kirk had greeted Gary with "Boy, Daddy, I was about to starve for some meat and potatoes. I'm glad you are home!"

Keith was in the high chair having a glorious time feeding himself bits of meat and potatoes. He looked up long enough for his meat-juice-stained face to grin that precious five-tooth grin. He swung one leg in display of happiness and pleasure and continued eating.

The boys were still a bit weak from the exposure to the virus by the vaccine. They didn't fuss about taking naps.

This weekend had seemed longer than usual since the boys were ill. There wasn't church to refresh the boys or me. I hadn't even taken time from my constant working to read from the Bible. Later after talking with my husband for a while, I cleaned the refrigerator and washed some clothes. I hung one load of clothes outside to dry. The next load was placed on a drying rack in the hall before the furnace in the way of the hall to the bathroom door. What can you do when it looks like rain and the clothes you need are damp feeling? I knew that the clothes would be needed by the boys in the morning. Gary always complained when I had to dry clothes in the hall. They really were in the way. This time I thought it was necessary.

After the evening meal, Gary was studying. I decided since the regular work for Art I was completed I would plan out the final form of the Christmas Elementary Music Program. It was two months away.

"This seems a long way off, but December fifteenth will be here before I know it," I said aloud, defending my planning.

"Seems wise to me," Gary complimented. "How many students will be in the program for the December Parent Teachers Organization meeting?"

"Well, I suppose all the children through sixth grade. Let me see, that is about 462 students," I quickly totaled the grade school enrollment of Nettelton Public Schools to get the number.

"Is anyone helping you?" Gary asked.

"Of course, Honey, the teachers do. Any parent I have asked to help has helped or gotten someone else to," I stated thankfully. "When is that test in your European History Class?"

"Next Tuesday," he said.

"Are you ready?" I inquired.

"I'm going to ace it. I think I know almost everything now," Gary assured me.

"When is the first basketball game?" I asked for at least the third time in three weeks. I couldn't seem to remember the date.

"Honestly, I've told you we are not finished with football. It will be the fourth Friday in November before we can play. It is an away game for the fourth time," he stated in a sharp tone of voice sounding irritated.

I apoligized, "Sorry, the days kind of run together on me since I'm home so much at night. Maybe I will be able to remember this time."

I'm studying, remember?" he let me know to be quiet.

I went to him and kissed him. "I remember," I said gently, returning to my work.

The evening was far spent. We were sleeping. The house was filled with the sounds of the air compressor. The laundry hung on the wooden drying rack in the hall before the return air vent of the furnace. We were unaware that the pilot light had gone out on the furnace about twelve midnight.

From the night sounds I hear, "Mom, Momma! Wake up! I'm cold again."

"What?" I said half asleep. I was unable to fully register the words. My night had only begun an hour and a half earlier. Soon the horror of the words struck me.

"Keith is crying! I'm cold again! Really cold this time!" Kirk said loudly.

"Get in bed! Gary, that furnace must be off again. Please wake up! The furnace!" I called to my sleepy husband. I shivered as I went to get Keith in a run.

Gary was up almost as soon as I was. With the familiarity of rousing ourselves quickly, neither of us required more than a few seconds to go from sleep to action.

Keith was like a lump of ice. I took a blanket and dry diaper with me back to my bed.

Dry clothes would help to stop Keith from crying.

"Poor baby!", I said feeling that maybe the clothes drying had some way caused the pilot light to go out, "Mommie is sorry."

Gary said angrily, "Why did the furnace go off? They came again, didn't they?"

"There were no clothes before!" I said exposing my guilt feeling, "Maybe the clothes did it?"

"Don't be silly. The clothes couldn't have caused it to go out the last time or this time," he rebuffed strongly.

"Yes, I suppose you are right. Keith is awfully cold. Should I take all his clothes off other than a diaper and put him next to me to warm him quickly?" I sought help.

"I'll get Kirk warmed. Do what you think is best. I'm angry!" he stated sharply.

Obviously he was angry. I drew the shivering baby next to my skin and covered him as much with my body as I could to warm him quickly. He was quaking with shivers. He soon stopped crying and settled down to sleep.

Quietly I questioned Gary, "Why didn't I wake up before they got so cold?"

"Because I was keeping you warm—remember?" Gary said warmly teasing. (I slept so close to him that he called me his second skin. For five and a half years he had kept me warm.)

"Oh hush," I rebuked.

The four of us slept until morning.

With the alarm clock our day started. Keith was changed and spot washed that morning so that I would not further chill his already weak body.

Gary had gotten up early too. He went to the maintenance department before class. He was stern enough with them so that the furnace was equipped with a new pilot apparatus before noon.

The boys began to run temperatures higher than normal.

Maggie told Gary at lunch, "Kirk has a temperature of 100 fahrenheit. Keith has 100.4 . What do we do?"

"Don't call Myrna," Gary cautioned. "We need to change antibiotics and start medication every three hours. The boys are to stay in bed or inactive. Give them lots of liquids. Mainly, try not to worry," Gary told Maggie and himself.

He had an important test tomorrow. That was enough pressure.

When I came home from school the temperatures were 102 and 102.4. Keith was still reacting more severly to the cold than Kirk. Certainly, I must call the doctor and confer with him.

"Doctor Kemp's office," Ruth said expectantly.

"Ruth, this is Myrna. We have a problem due to a sudden change in temperature in our house last night. I need to talk to the doctor."

"You can talk with him in a few minutes. He is with a patient right now," she informed me.

I waited. In a few minutes I heard the doctor say, "Myrna, are the boys wheezing or what?"

"They have no symptoms other than fever right now. Did Ruth tell you what happened?" I asked.

"She told me that a change in temperature occurred, yes. That was all. Why? What did happen?" he inquired further.

"The furnace went off. The boys were ice cold when Kirk woke me. They didn't run fever the last time this happened. Could this be a second reaction to the flu vaccine? What do I do beside the usual?" I asked and stated rapidly because of the perplexity I felt.

"Yes, it could be a reaction to the virus since they are not wheezing or coughing more than usual. Try to calm down and relax or you will have high blood pressure," he stated calmly and wisely.

"What are you doing for the boys now?" the doctor inquired, treating his patients to good counsel.

I took a deep breath and said, "We have changed to Tetracycline once each three hours starting at lunch time today. I have fixed chicken broth to get some nourishment into them and juice to keep the fluid level up. They are drinking juice each hour or more often if they are awake. Both boys are in bed or lying down constantly."

"What are their temperatures and when did they start?" he demanded professionally.

"Kirk has 102 and Keith has 102.4," I stated in the same professional way, "and they started running fever about lunch time."

"If this is a second flu reaction they will probably be back to normal by Thursday. If they have temperatures beyond 103 you call me. I don't care what time. Call me at home if you need to. Understand?" the doctor stated.

"Yes," I replied, gratefully. His steady directions quieted some of my fear.

"Spread the antibiotic to a three and a half hour interval, using the usual dosage for each boy. I want to see the boys—if they are still ill on Friday," he concluded.

"Thank you, Doctor Kemp. I'll call you if the fever gets beyond the 103 mark," I assured.

Kirk was on the couch. He heard the end of the conversation. He was feeling badly, yet he was alert.

He asked, "Is 102 a bad fever, Mom?"

"You don't feel good do you?" I said trying to make light of the numbers.

"Will I have to go to the hospital? Will Keif?" he asked in a worried tone of voice.

"No, silly, you are only a little sick. Be a good boy and stay still so you can fight those germs that are making you sick," I assured him without the thought of my right to use the name of Jesus against those germs.

I took Kirk into my arms to assess if the temperature was stabilized or going up. He was feverish. I refrained from taking his temperature again. He needed rest and calm to get well. I must make him feel that I knew he would be well soon. I carried Kirk to his bed baby fashion talking baby talk to him. He laughed. I got more ice for the mist tent. Soon the hum of the motor lulled him to sleep. Keith was in his bed. He looked frail and ghostly white. I checked the flap of the mist tent to assure him some of the moist air. When they both slept I left the room. I was sick inside.

When I went back to the living room Maggie was sitting pensively. I forced the tears back and sat down on the couch. Unaware of what I was doing I pinched at the brown multicolored short loops of threads.

Maggie spoke, "Myrna, is this how most of the last three years have been?"

"Not really, at least not all the time. Are you sure you will be able to keep on helping us? Even if my sons are sick? We really need you. You're so very kind and good with the boys." I talked as sort of a filler. She was necessary and I did want her to stay, but more than that I wanted the boys to live. Now my hopes were very shakey. I was having a hard time just believing the boys would overcome their temperatures.

"You need me more than anyone I have ever worked for. Of course, I'll keep on helping you," Maggie assured.

"Oh, dear, I had better call the school to get a substitute for tomorrow!" I said to Maggie and myself.

As I was making the call, Maggie left for the day.

My mind raged within me. Soon my comfort came when I prayed, "Father, help me! I'm scared, and tired. Help me!" In my mind instantly I remembered a scripture I had memorized years before.

"The earth is the Lord's, and they that dwell therein." (Psalm 24:I para.)

Then another bit came to mind.

"Come unto me all ye that labor and are heavy laden and I will give you rest." (Matt. 11:28)

I reasoned, He didn't promise an easy burden. Yet, I did expect a yolk that fit well. Precious to me would have been the news that the Lord doesn't give burdens.

Monday night I was up almost all the time. The boys' fever stabilized at 102° early in the morning. When they had gone beyond 102.5° I had bathed the backs of their necks with a cold wash cloth. The fever was doing its work, killing viruses. Too high a fever was bad, but this much was making my sons well.

At seven in the morning both the boys had 102.4° of fever.

I called the school. "This is Myrna. Surprise, I'll be at work today. You can have the substitute for someone else."

"We need one too. The boys are better?" the secretary asked caringly.

"No, the same. I can't do anything here except worry and maybe give some tender loving care. Maggie is good at TLC. I'll be at work. Bye." I said.

At lunch time I called Maggie. "Maggie, do I need to come home? Are the temps down?"

"We are less feverish, yes. I'm worried about energy. May I feed them?" Maggie inquired.

"If they want to eat, feed them. Fruits would be best. Probably you need to give enzymes too. They should be awfully hungry," I surmised.

"Are you O.K.?" Maggie asked, knowing I was awake all night.

"I'm working. I guess that means I'm O.K.," I said without feeling.

"See you this afternoon. I have to go now," I said realizing class was about to begin.

"Bye," Maggie said terminating the conversation.

"Maggie, did she say we could eat?" Kirk asked. He was hungry. He lay on the couch watching television.

"You can if you are hungry."

"Oh boy! Could I have some jello? Please?" Kirk asked.

"Of course, you may. I'll fix some right now," she said happily as she walked toward the kitchen.

Kirk was ready to begin eating. The fever was beginning to leave his body. He was very weak, but gaining in spirit. The warm, sweet, good-tasting jello refreshed him even more.

"Gee thanks, Maggie, that was really good," he said sincerely, licking his lips.

When I came home from school I found the still-feverish Kirk resting on the couch. Maggie held Keith. She was giving him some juice and a few bites of apple sauce with enzymes.

"Myrna, I think the boys are doing better than they were this morning," Maggie assessed. "Their temperatures were down some at lunch time."

"What are they now? Shall I take them?" I offered.

"I suppose we should," Maggie agreed.

The boys obediently took turns having their temperatures taken under their arms. The temperature there always registered one degree below the actual temperature by mouth. I added the degree. Then I spoke to all of us.

"The temperatures say Kirk is better and Keith is still a sick little boy," I told the three.

"Mom, I still feel bad!" Kirk said emphasizing the bad.

"Keith would probably say the same thing," I added, "if he could tell us."

"Maggie, thank you for being willing to stay with the boys when they are ill. I really needed time away from them. I can see things more in perspective when I am away for a while."

Thursday, as the doctor had predicted, the boys were back to normal temperatures. The sincere, warm pediatrician had faith in the exactness with which his instructions would be followed by us. He preferred the boys to stay at home so long as oxygen or other special medical procedures were not needed. The boys were secure and well-cared-for here. For them to visit the hospital was possible exposure to microbes. He felt they did not need to chance contact like that unless it was absolutely necessary. We had an agreement with him and understood these things.

I reported to Doctor Kemp on Friday. The boys were better. I was apprehensive about taking them, yet I felt the doctor must see them.

The three of us entered the doctor's office.

"Hello Ruth, we are here," I stated happily.

"Are you much better?" Ruth asked Kirk.

"Yep!" Kirk affirmed.

"Yes Ma'am, thank you," Kirk restated.

"Keith is still very weak," I confided.

"I would be, too," Ruth said sympathetically.

The visit was a general check up for the boys. Temperatures were normal. Both of the boys had lost weight. Kirk weighed one pound less than one week ago. Keith was one-half pound lighter.

Ruth took the boys back into the lobby so the doctor could talk to me.

"Myrna, Keith is very much underweight. His stomach is swollen with malnutrition. I want your permission to send him to the University Medical Center in Little Rock. They have an excellent staff and program specializing in cystic fibrosis study. I will make the arrangements for him to be studied there. What do you say? They should be able to help us out by putting some pounds on Keith." The doctor looked at me when he had finished.

I stared into space. Hospital—oh no! I don't want to send my tiny son away. Yet, maybe they could help. I want him to live. It doesn't look like he will here with what we are able to do for him.

I heard myself say, "I'll have to talk to Gary. As much as I don't want to do this—you are right. He will not live through the winter this way. I know that. You know that I do. Gary knows too. I'll talk with him tonight."

Tears started in my eyes, but they didn't flow. I seldom cried. The pain of seeing Keith each day was my quiet, guilty burden. If only I didn't have this strange genetic gift to bequeath death to my children instead of life. My guilt was deep within and often I thought of it in torturously twisted dreams or in flashes of Keith's body during the day. As I lifted myself from the chair, I said to the doctor, "Please, *do not* give cystic fibrosis children flu shots. Let them take the chance of not being exposed to the virus at all. Fighting it the best they can naturally surely would be better. My boys didn't need the suffering they have had this week."

He did not speak at first. Then he quietly said, "You are probably right, Myrna. I was advised to give them."

Sensing his sincerity, I said gently, "Thank you for being willing to come out anytime. That means a lot to me."

The weather was pleasant. The boys were better and being out in the sunshine made them happy.

I asked teasingly, "Would anybody like a Dairy Queen ice cream cone?"

"I would! Keif says he would too," Kirk said nodding his head vigorously giving a joyful majority vote.

"Okay, we will have some ice cream," I stated happily pushing the thoughts of hospital from my mind.

We stopped at the tiny Dairy Queen shop. I left the auto. When I had purchased the small cones I returned. I held Keith so he could eat his cone.

"Kirk, be careful! Ice cream is good, but remember it is drippy," I warned as the cone was tipped dangerously sideward.

"Boy Mom, look at Keif. He has eaten more ice cream than me!" Kirk said affirming the correctness of his vote.

"He surely has," I confirmed.

Keith looked up with a twinkle in his encircled eyes.

"That's a good boy. Enjoy your ice cream," I stated in a complimentary way. I hugged my son warmly. My heart was nearly breaking with the thought of his going to the hospital. Surely, they will help him. I must keep thinking that. He nestled close to me as though he understood the hurt in my heart. Oh, the pain of this genetic thing!

On the outside I laughed and smiled at my children. Within was the hurt of the parent with a genetic lethal, seeing her children dying with the traits' symptoms. Knowing you were the source for a child's disease was a pain of the soul for which I had no understanding nor relief. It was a fact. I didn't know any way to change it, so I had to accept it. It seemed there was no one to blame. It was just a curse from antiquity through the tiny genes. We were one of twenty. That was what the doctors had said. One out of every twenty whites from northern European ancestry had the trait. Gary and I were both one-in-twenties. What hurtful consequences.

4

Turkey and Terror

Gary hung the telephone with a limp hand.

"Maggie, Keith will be admitted to the University of Little Rock Medical Center next Tuesday, November 13th. I wish he didn't have to go," Gary said with a deep sadness in his voice.

"Will you take him to the hospital?" Maggie wondered.

"Myrna will have to take him. She doesn't need to drive those one-hundred-twenty-five miles alone with Keith. Let me think what we can do," Gary answered pensively.

"Charles Gwaltney has been most helpful. Why don't you call him?" Maggie wisely advised.

Gary walked back to the kitchen and began dialing the familiar number.

Gary knew that he wanted to go with me but practice made his being away impossible. Kirk needed one of his parents during the beginning of the separation, too. Gary felt a strong sadness because he realized that the best we could do was not enough. Keith was getting weaker and thinner. The pain of seeing Keith like this was causing him to ache inside. Gary spent his energy in basketball and in studying. He filled his time so that there was little time for dwelling on the pain he felt. He loved his sons. He wanted his sons. They had gotten from him something he had no idea he had, cystic fibrosis. He hurt. The pain showed in his walk and in his face.

If I explained once I explained a hundred times that Keith would have to go to the hospital in Little Rock so they could help him gain some weight and get stronger. After almost an hour of explaining to Kirk, Gary came in the door from basketball practice just in time to keep me from getting totally out of patience.

"Oh, thank God you're home! Kirk just can't seem to understand why Keith has to go to the hospital," I said as Gary just barely got inside the door.

Kirk looked questioningly at Gary and asked, "Why does Keif have to go to the hospital? He doesn't have 'monia."

Kirk looked steadfastly for a better answer from his father.

"Son, your mother has told you why. Doctor Kemp thinks they can help him gain some weight," Gary told Kirk more optimistically than he felt.

"Daddy, when will he come home?" Kirk asked innocently.

"Soon, we hope," Gary said.

I looked at the frail child in my arms. I felt the hopelessness both of us had experienced for several months. Tears came into my eyes. Keith coughed repeatedly with a deep, racking croupy sound. We had grown accustomed to the grotesque, soul-cutting sound. I looked at his little fingers. They were thickened at the ends from lack of oxygen and poor circulation. My eyes traveled to the chest that curved outward like Kirk's. Staying alive was a daily ordeal for my tiny son. I patted him as I swayed my arms from side to side cradling him.

Tuesday was a pleasant, sunny day. My arrangements for a substitute teacher were completed the day before. Now I was dressed and so was Keith. I looked at him and smiled. He was a beautiful baby in his red corduroy suit. He looked at me with sad brown eyes. I could feel him watch me as I completed the preparations for our leaving. He blinked his long brown eyelashed eyelids as he patiently followed me from the bedroom, to the living room then back to the kitchen. His gaze never left me as I gathered all the things he needed for his stay at the hospital.

Presently, at exactly six-thirty, the woman Charles arranged to take us to Little Rock turned in our driveway. We left quietly without making much noise so that we thought we had not wakened Kirk or Gary. I was numb with the horror of having to leave my baby in the hospital. I wasn't sure I would ever see him alive again. "I love you, Baby," I said to Keith as I cried to myself. Keith sensed my anxiety. He snuggled close to me as I carried him to the car.

Within me was the realization that I had not dared to love this child with the total abandon that I adored my first-born. Perhaps it was due to the fact that at two weeks of age I had realized that he, too, had symptoms of cystic fibrosis. The fact that I was now taking him to a hospital made me realize that my reserved affections were somewhat in self-defense. The heavy feeling inside of me made me realize for the first time just how strongly I had grown to love this never complaining child. Could I really leave this tiny, ill child that far from home alone? I had not wanted to. There was no choice. If I didn't return to work there would be no money to live on. I had to do this. I must. There was only a small talk exchange with this kind woman. Mostly, I thought and held my child to me more tenderly and lovingly than ever before. This was the last chance to let him know that I wanted to help him get well because I loved him. Finally, becoming aware of the strain on my hostess because of my silence, I began conversing with Mrs. Burk.

When we neared Little Rock Keith began to cough to the point of retching. Mrs. Burk grimaced at the sound.

"Please, find a place to get off the highway and stop!" I emphatically directed.

"Soon, or do we have a bit of time?" she asked.

"Right now, please, please hurry!" I blurted out quickly concerned with trying to get Keith's choking under control. My efforts failed. He had gotten very warm and was near vomiting.

She stopped the car quickly. I opened the door just in time to prevent Keith from messing up her auto. He retched. His breakfast was lost. He was weakly crying with the stress of the ordeal. I wiped his forehead with a wet wash cloth.

"Myrna," she asked sadly, "does this happen often?"

"Yes, very often. That's why we just have to try the hospital." I answered sadly with tears welling into my eyes.

"I just couldn't see how you could leave him in the hospital until now. I think I've begun to understand," she said sadly and with tears in her eyes.

We entered the back of the University of Little Rock Medical Center. The lobby and waiting area was huge. I went to the nurse at a podium-type desk. She asked the usual type questions to get the information she needed. I answered politely. When she had completed the questions I asked where I might wait in a private area because Keith had cystic fibrosis.

The nurse told me, "there is no private area. You will wait here, like everyone else."

I pleaded, "But, my baby has cystic fibrosis. He can't wait here. He'll catch something."

My plea fell on deaf ears. She shrugged and continued with the next patient.

It was nine-thirty. Mrs. Burk had gone to visit a friend in another part of the hospital. I selected the end of a couch so I didn't have to be near anyone who was coughing. Fear of the waiting room almost caused me to scream. I thought of waiting outside, but I feared the cold and not being taken in as soon as possible. Each time an orderly or nurse passed I told them about Keith. I begged for special privileges for my baby. The time passed slowly. At about eleven o'clock a Graduate Registered Nurse passed as I was changing one of Keith's foul smelling diapers. Some other patients had moved away from us during this time. I smiled to myself about the ill-gotten space. At least, I thought, the bad smell will keep people away. It did except the R.N. She came over to me.

"Does your baby have cystic fibrosis?" she asked. "I couldn't miss the odor."

I nodded my head yes in reply and continued, "Please, have mercy. I'm horrified he may catch something here. He's very weak."

"Come with me," she directed leading the way to her office.

I followed after gathering my belongings. The expanse of windows were at my back as I walked toward the row of room dividers within which were a row of open-topped offices. She opened the locked door for us. I silently thanked God.

At eleven-forty-five we were summoned to the pediatrics admitting area. Ten minutes later a nurse took Keith and his things from my arms. Keith disappeared through a door. I stood near tears, and was led to a doctor's office.

The doctor introduced himself and interviewed me. I was asked questions about my sons, then family and personal feelings in connection with cystic fibrosis. My subconscious mind must have been carrying me through the interview, for I heard myself answer his questions.

We left Keith. It was twelve-thirty. We found our way out of the hospital. As we drove across Little Rock I made effort to memorize my way from the hospital east through the city. I wanted to know exactly how to get the car back to the hospital in case Keith needed me quickly.

At the edge of the city we stopped at a small cafe. I ate, but the food had no taste to me. Mrs. Burk and I conversed on many typical conversation topics. We continued the exchange on the way home. Mostly, I asked questions so I could think while she answered. I needed to regain my inner composure and face having left my baby in the hospital.

Soon she stopped the auto in front of our home. I turned toward my house. The house looked the same, yet I knew it would never be the same. Keith wasn't there. Looking at my watch as I entered the door I noted it was four o'clock.

Kirk ran to me and grabbed me around the left leg. The octopus cried out, "Mommie!"

"Hi, Baby! Did you have a good day?" I asked as I lifted Kirk into my arms.

"Yep! I woke Daddy up! It was fun!" Kirk assured.

I saw the scene in my mind, and said without my usual enthusiasm, "I'm glad."

Maggie could see the tiredness in me, "Kirk hasn't taken a nap."

"Things were kind of unsettling. Come on take a nap with me," I said inviting my son with a loving hug.

"You need some lovin', Mom?" Kirk asked walking toward the bedroom.

"Yep, I guess I do," I confessed as we walked hand in hand to the master bedroom. "Will you pat me? Night Maggie."

Kirk slept soundly within a short time. I lay thinking. My in-laws were upset that I was not staying with Keith. I was upset, too. Money, I thought, you necessary stuff. The needs for it forced me to work. Gary paid for school with basketball and I fed us. I must work all the days I can so we could try to pay for the hospital bill. We dreaded the figure. Blue Cross had long ago dismissed the boys from coverage on the 'Family' policy. We tithed and believed that God would supply, but with our commonsense we tried to figure out how. Gary and I had discussed our feelings. We felt trapped, guilty, and frustrated by the financial and personal responsibility.

There was a certain feeling of uncertainty and sadness in our home. Kirk sensed this change. However, he was able to play with Kevin often which made him less lonely. Kevin lived across the back yard. Their friendship grew. Both the boys needed to play. They had fun. Part of their fun was discussing what they wanted Santa Claus to bring them. Donna and I listened as the boys talked. Often we could hear Kirk dreaming of a red Farmall riding tractor. He told us about it often.

I wrote to my mother-in-law regularly. We were different, but much alike in our strength of determination. We loved and respected each other deeply. I told Lola what Kirk wanted. Without our knowing it, Lola began making it a reality. She and Grandpa Dude placed an order for the tractor.

Days went by almost as usual until I looked into the empty little bed. We called the hospital at least twice a week to inquire about Keith. On Thursday they told us that he had pneumonia and had been running fever for several days. There was no way I could leave for Little Rock before Saturday. We prayed for God's help and courage.

The days of the week and a half were almost over. After days of anguish and prayer I entered our Chevrolet for my trip to see Keith.

"Tell Mom bye, Kirk," I heard Gary instruct after he had properly kissed me goodbye. He always told each of us, his books in hand, goodbye each morning as we left for school. Any failure in this routine caused him to cry bitterly.

"Bye Mom. Tell Keif I miss him," Kirk added as he threw an additional kiss to me.

"Goodbye Darlings. I'll be back early in the afternoon tomorrow."

Driving from Newport, Arkansas over the railroad yard I looked at the water-filled ditches conducting the rain water toward the White River. The bridges were on levy type fills that placed the road nearly twenty-five feet above the water and land level. Driving on the fill always gave me the feeling of flying. I glanced at the speedometer and steadied the marker on seventy miles an hour. This Saturday was a lonely time for me. Though the sun was shining, I was feeling helpless and empty. I wanted this visit with Keith, but I dreaded what I might find at the hospital.

At the hospital, I identified myself and told the nurse, "I've come to visit my son Keith in bed one."

She replied with compassion, "He isn't in bed one. He had pneumonia and was placed in bed eight in isolation."

She directed me down the hall to the left of where I had left Keith one and a half weeks earlier.

The children in the ward were visible through the unique glass walls. Soon I saw bed eight. As I entered the room I recoiled with terror. There lay a child in his diaper, in a tent attached to a vapor and oxygen regulating machine. I hardly recognized him. His throat was covered with a rash stained red by methiolate. There was an intravenous tube attached to one of his toes. The frail body was reduced even more so that the flesh hung from his bones. Tears came into my eyes as my son opened his eyes. I went under the tent with him. He cried a frail, pitiful cry. I talked to him gently. He stopped the soft yet wailing crying and looked directly at me. I touched the tiny arms as he responded to my voice, face and touch. He seemed to relax some. In a few minutes, I could no longer bear to stay in the tent without crying. I withdrew from under the tent and looked at the first page of the chart which was hung on a hook at the foot of the bed.

"Allergy to methylate" was written across the preliminary page. I noted the antibiotics used. He was critically ill. I knew it without looking at the chart. The pain I felt in my heart told me to get ready for the inevitable. He would die soon, as we had thought, and accepted.

I went to the nurse and asked, "When is my baby to be fed?"

"The bottles are prepared. The food cart should be here very soon. Do you want to feed him?" she questioned.

"Yes, I definitely want to feed him. May I hold him?" I asked meekly.

"He has not eaten well or slept normally since he arrived," she said curtly in accusation of my absence.

"There was no choice but for me to leave him. My husband is a college student working his way through college by playing basketball. What I earn is all the income we have, and at home my three and a half-year old son has cystic fibrosis."

My self-defense broke her indignation. "Oh," she replied "I'm sorry. I didn't know."

"I love him yet, obviously he will not be able to survive much longer," I confessed without emotion in my voice.

Holding was like heaven. He was always a sweet, non-complaining child. Even now he nursed some of the enriched formula. He was so weak that I held him gently and stroked his brown hair. The baby hair wasn't completely replaced in the front. He was a handsome child. He had a prominent nose and well shaped chin. He had large eyebrows with beautiful long eyelashes. They were sunken somewhat with the weight loss. His shoulders were much broader than his head. They were even from his birth. My thoughts of death held me captive, yet I too napped as I held my swaddled, skeletal son. The nurse came in to give him medication. His upper thigh was the only remaining skeletal muscle large enough to accomodate the antibiotics. Keith gave out a feeble scream. I experienced a desire to scream too.

Later, when he had settled down the nurse came in and said gently, "He needs the oxygen tent again."

"All right," I said as I moved to take him back to his bed. Keith was content to sleep.

In the waiting room I sat down. After coming to my senses I realized that I was hungry. I hadn't eaten anything since I fixed breakfast early in the morning.

In the cafeteria I joined some of the staff at a table and found their conversation interesting and temporarily forgot my problems. Later I went to the lounge in the medical school classroom structure. In the middle of the lounge area was a beautiful baby grand piano. I walked toward the lovely creation and assessed its availability. "May I play?" I asked simply of a student. "Sure," was the reply.

Cystic fibrosis wasn't the only genetic problem in our family. Since childhood my ability to memorize music or any other sequence was impaired. I thought, there is a piano. I haven't any music. What can I recall?

Only one melody flowed. "Nobody knows the trouble I've seen, Nobody knows my sorrow, Nobody knows the trouble I've seen, Glory, Hallelujah..." Tears dropped involuntarily as I played through the

old spiritual. Presently, the peace that passed understanding returned to me. God is in control, I didn't
understand, but I knew it was true.

Later, I returned to Keith's room.

He wasn't breathing. I called for help. There was a
scurrying about as they came from other areas of
service to assist. I hurried out of the room. I walked
and prayed at the same time.

Keith lay near death.

The doctors were irritated by the questioning I put
to them. Even though I asked several questions after
they did an E.K.G., they really knew nothing to tell
me. Finally, I was allowed back into the room with
Keith. He was sleeping or in a coma. I couldn't tell
which for sure.

He seemed stabilized, so I waited the hour then I
called home.

After the call I began to think about where I might
rest. The horror of the experience just past dulled my
senses. The day seemed longer than the seventeen
hours that had passed. It was 11 p.m.

One of the interns said, "Are you staying here
tonight?"

"Yes," I replied, "in this chair, call me if anything
else happens."

"Well, I won't be on duty but come with me. I want
to show you a place to rest."

I followed, grateful for the kindness.

"This is the study room for the interns. No one will
be here tonight. This recliner will be more restful for
you than that chair," he stated truthfully. "There are
books to read, if you can't sleep."

My sleep was fitful. Several times I wakened
during the night to checking on my son. At six
o'clock I again went to Keith's bed to see that he was
being fed intravenously. He couldn't be taken out of
bed to be fed, or held. I talked to him and patted him.
The tears started and a sick feeling of helplessness

engulfed me. Also I was remembering some of the pictures from one of the medical books on genetic diseases of children. The faceless, grotesque, pitiful bodies of other victims of genetic lethals lurked in my mind. The faces were covered to protect the innocent? Keith was to be one of those pictures. We had agreed to let him be used as a teaching case. How could I? Quickly, I left his side and went by the nurses' counter.

I cried as I left the hospital, yet I couldn't do anything here. I was needed at home. My thoughts cancelled any hope of life for Keith. Circumstances convinced me my son would die soon.

The world didn't know my inner turmoil. It thought I looked well, happy, maybe even pretty in the white wool dress with gold trim at the neck. My blond hair shifted in the cool breeze that came in through the slightly lowered window to allow the antiseptic smell of the hospital to leave my nostrils. Where was illness? Where was death? How does God see me? Am I a foreigner to Him, like death is to life? There was little Biblical basis to the thoughts I was entertaining. My faith was there that He was in control, but I didn't understand anything about getting what faith I had to grow. Instead there were thoughts from the enemy. I could kill myself on the way home. It would likely be thought an accident. Now that would be really stinky. Where would that leave Gary? He would have two sick sons and a dead wife. I'm to depend on God to sustain me no matter what happens. Besides, suicide is really murder of yourself. I can't ignore God's rules. Murder is wrong! My inner spirit or self reminded me gently.

The battle within me continued to rage. My inner self saying God is able and the enemy saying just hit one of those bridges. Let everyone else tough it out. Think about yourself. You're always giving. No, you can't do that. Think about Kirk and Gary. What about Myrna? I've been with death all night. Why not join Keith? He's going to die. I know he is. Finally, I said aloud, "I must do what is best for everyone, not just the easy way out for me."

Then I began to hum, "Nobody Knows" and the tears started to flow. I slowed the auto to fifty-five miles an hour and continued singing, "A Mighty Fortress is Our God."

The mental anguish had subsided and thoughts of school, surroundings and other normal thoughts again occupied my mind. I thought of dinner and Thanksgiving with our families. I was glad to be alive. And I was happy I had chosen not to try to kill myself. "Home, here I come, ready or not!" I said aloud as I thought about dinner.

As I went through the hospital trial, Gary and Kirk stayed at home expecting visitors. Gary put on a roast. He was thankful his parents had been generous with the meat from their farm. There were potatoes from the garden of my parents. He was counting his blessings.

A bit later, at eleven o'clock, an Arkansas State Highway Trouper came to the door of our house. He knocked on the door.

Gary greeted him filled with apprehension. "Yes Sir?" he asked.

Are you Gary?" he asked.

"Yes Sir, I am." A twinge of fear in his voice yet he wanted to get to the business at hand.

"There's been an accident," the man tried to be direct, but the severity of the news made him hesitate. "Near Blytheville your dad and mother were in an accident. They are in the Blytheville Hospital seriously injured. Why don't you sit down, Sir. I'm very sorry." He was forcing Gary to sit down before the shock fully registered.

Kirk watched and went to his father who sat stunned, thinking what to do. "Grandpa and Grandma are hurt?" he asked trying to understand.

"Yes, Son," Gary said not believing the words he heard himself saying.

"Do you want me to take you?" the officer asked kindly.

"Kirk can't stay alone. Let me think. I'll get the neighbors next door to stay with Kirk. And I want to call the church to have them pray for my parents." Gary planned wisely.

He made the call. Next he went next door. The kindly neighbors came back with him right then.

He told Kirk, "You be a good boy. Your Mom will be home soon. Mind now!" After a kiss and hug he left.

My parents drove into the driveway after Gary had been gone a short while. The neighbors told them of the accident. Grandpa Lou decided to go back to where they had seen a bad accident near Blytheville. He left.

Grandma Goehri took Kirk into her arms and loved him. She realized the crushed auto they had passed at Blytheville was the same accident. She gave Kirk a feeling of security and calm. She was praying for strength inside her mind. She played with Kirk as they waited and prayed for God's help for Dude, Lola, Gary and the family. The telephone rang.

"Hello."

"Honey, it was the accident we saw. Dude is dead and Lola is in the hospital here. I think they are going to send her to Memphis. Gary's going to stay with her. I'll be back after awhile. Are you O.K.?"

"I think so," she answered limply, and began to cry.

"Grandpa is dead?" Kirk asked.

"Yes, Kirk, a car hit Grandpa's car and Grandpa Dude is in heaven." She assured, "Grandma Lola is hurt, but with the Lord's help, she'll be well again soon."

Kirk was thinking. He knew what happened to George and Harry. Grandpa Dude was dead. Kirk began to cry. "Grandpa is dead? Like George and Harry?" he asked trying to understand, "Like that?"

"Yes, Sweetheart like George and Harry."

They continued lamenting together. Kirk's grandmother's faith was strong. It comforted both of them. In awhile Kirk resorted to the reality of his body. "Boy, Grandma, could we eat? I'm really hungry."

As they ate, she asked Kirk, "When is your mom supposed to be home?"

"Lunch time. Keif has 'monia. Mom told Daddy last night that he's really sick." Kirk informed without understanding the gravity of his remarks.

The hours passed very slowly. Waiting always seems longer than work she thought.

"Where are the cars?" I said aloud as I drove into the driveway. By now everyone should be here. Wonder what's going on.

Kirk popped from the door. "Mom, Grandpa is dead!"

"Which Grandpa?" I blurted, not really understanding the impact of his statement.

"Grandpa Dude is dead!" he repeated, "and Grandma is hurt bad!"

As he finished, I whisped him into my arms. By then Mom was out of the door.

"Oh, God help! Mom, when? where? and where is Gary?"

The rest of my homecoming welcome blended into a mass of benumbed and non-feeling responses. I didn't even say "hello" or hug my mother until later.

Inside the house I sank onto the couch and said after the shock subsided, "Keith almost died last night. How much can we take?" This time I sobbed holding Kirk as he tried to comfort me by patting me.

Then silence. We simply couldn't talk. Kirk and Mother went outside for awhile. There were a few telephone calls asking how we were. I was calm essentially, and told them so. Repeating the morose details of the day seemed like some story from a morbid book that really wasn't happening to us. My mind was shaken by the sudden untimely accident. My mother and dad had called Gary's parents to try to come down to visit with them. By God's providence of mercy they missed Gary's parents by only a few minutes. What if both sets of parents were in the hospital today, or worse, dead? Energy came into me when I realized God was all present and really loved me, even in this mess.

Kirk popped in the door, "Mom, are you hungry? I am."

"Come in. We'll eat." We ate with little talk. Only Kirk enjoyed the food. Mother and I ate because we knew we needed the energy the food would give.

About four o'clock my father returned. He walked in and hugged me. He had regained his usual steadiness. "They've taken Lola to the Baptist Hospital in Memphis for intensive care and surgery—if she lives." His voice cracked on the last part.

"That bad?" I asked unbelieving.

"Yes," he replied feeling helpless.

Kirk stayed very quiet and leaned close to me. We prepared to stay the night in Jonesboro.

In the morning we packed the autos and went to meet Gary at the mortuary in Blytheville. The date of the funeral was uncertain, because it was Gary's Uncle's desire that they not have the funeral until Lola could be told that Dude was dead. When we arrived at Blytheville the reality of the accident was suddenly ugly, violently alive. Gary was very upset. His dad had been on the shoulder of the road when a man, just having left a bar drove head on into the driver's side of their car. His dad had died instantly. His mother had evidently been asleep. Her head and face and right arm were badly broken.

We sobbed together. Not really wise enough to really help each other through the mourning. Neither of us had ever mourned for someone really important before.

Kirk loved seeing his cousins. But with all of the upsets the time passed slowly even for him. We spent time between Memphis and Benton, Missouri. Lola had surgery on Wednesday. She had been unable to be told of Dude's death yet. The doctor had told them that the shock might kill her. The days of darkness passed slowly. We prayed for Lola and accepted calls of condolences for Dude. Everyone who came to the funeral home to view Dude asked of Lola. They were loved greatly by their neighbors.

At the funeral home I noticed Kirk peaking as often as he dared out into the parlor. He watched us as we were being comforted.

Finally I noticed him and walked slowly to him. "What are you looking for?" I asked in a soft, sad voice. "Grandpa's funeral," Kirk admitted, "but, where is it? I couldn't see it." Kirk was confused.

"Grandpa's body is in there in the big thing. It's called a coffin. The flowers and people who liked Grandpa are here to tell us people will miss him." I tried to adequately explain, but how do you explain a funeral to a three year old? In my mind I prayed for help. "Grandpa is in heaven," I continued, "but people can't go to heaven when they want to, so they come to his funeral. A funeral is the people, flowers and Grandpa's family—all together." I paused. We looked at each other. He was thinking. "Do you understand?" I asked gently and seriously.

Kirk nodded yes and asked, "Can I go out there?"

Together we viewed the funeral. Kirk had begun to understand the finality of death.

Dude was buried Thursday in the Garden of Memories in a plot the grandparents had bought thinking of Keith.

Later we went to Memphis to see Lola, then home. Being home helped put death back into perspective for me.

Gary had been to Memphis twice to see his mother. She had extensive facial surgery early in the week. She was gaining strength. We had prayed only for her to recover. Never had we even thought she might not live. We refused to think that!

Friday Kirk was at home with Maggie.

Keith remained seriously ill and alone in the hospital in Little Rock. Gary was to play in the first home game of the season on Saturday night. There were two loved ones in the hospital we wanted to visit.

It seemed strange that the turkey of Thanksgiving had been obscured by the terror of the accident and Keith's stay in the hospital. Thanksgiving hadn't been the usual time of family joy and giving of thanks for blessings. We were almost unaware of the passing of the day.

5

The Christmas Tractor

Lola continued to improve. We kept in touch with the family who were staying in the hospital with her. The surgery was successful. She recovered steadily. However, she had not been strong enough to be told of her husband's death. Now she knew without having been told.

Saturday, after checking on Keith we decided to go to Memphis to see Lola. We found her rational, concerned for her grandchild, and we were thankful for the drastic improvement.

Sunday, December 1st the telephone rang. I heard, "This is the University Medical Center. Your son, Keith Alan, is dead." The voice paused. I began to cry, "When did it happen?" I heard an answer, but it didn't register in my mind.

There were few tears left. The three of us huddled together. How do you accept so much loss so quickly? We reasoned. Keith was not suffering the nightmare I remembered. That was it. We had to think on the things that were good about the loss, not for ourselves, but for the person who left us. He would never have to grow old. He wouldn't have to cough anymore. He wasn't frail, nor did he have to hurt anymore. The hurt was buried for me. I refused to mourn. My son had entered the eternal. He was there with his grandfather and all the rest of the family of God.

We thought of Lola. "How will we tell her?" Gary asked our question.

"She'll know. Remember, she knew your dad was gone." I was correct she had known and she sensed this loss too.

After a few telephone calls we left for Sikeston. Momma greeted us at the door. I could tell she had been crying. She was comforted when she realized we had accepted what had happened. She knew we thought it inevitable that Keith would die. Keith was in heaven.

In a little while we went to Welsh's Funeral Home. Keith was handsome in the sweater and cap that we had bought for him. My imagination made his face contort into a cry. I fought off the memories of the last visit. Finally, my mind could let him rest in the sweet sleep of death. I cryed only for my loss, not for my son. He was much better off than I was.

Kirk came to the funeral home with his Dad Tuesday morning before the funeral. I took Kirk into my arms and began reiterating the funeral and death. Everyone left us alone as I began to explain.

"Kirk, this isn't Keith," I stated.

"It isn't?" Kirk asked puzzled.

"No. It's only the shell where Keith used to live. He's in heaven with Grandpa and God."

"Mom, where's heaven?" Kirk asked expecting directions. He was staring at Keith's body in the child sized coffin.

"I don't know. I believe that I'll be there someday. God will take me there even though I don't know where it is."

"Mommy, when will Keith come back from heaven?"

"He won't come back. Someday we'll go to where he is. Everybody dies someday," I instructed softly. "Keith doesn't hurt anymore?" Kirk asked. "He doesn't have 'monia?" He was beginning to understand. As we stood there for the few minutes I nodded answers to his questions near tears as he wiped the tears off his cheeks. We both knew when we left that Keith was better off than before and we were relieved of the pain of his torture.

Then I said, "That's right. He doesn't hurt. There are no more coughs. He can run and grow and laugh with other children in heaven. But, he won't come home. This body is only where he used to live." I pointed to the vacant body. "Today we'll bury him, like we did George and Grandpa." I ceased talking and sobbed slightly along with Kirk. Today he learned more about the permanent state of death. Yet, we were experiencing the peace and hope of eternity with Jesus our Lord who paid the price for our hope.

"Momma, are the flowers Keith's funeral?" Kirk asked sadly, remembering the explanation from the previous week.

"Yes, sweetheart," I assured as I took Kirk toward the door and to his Grandma Carolyn. The two walked hand-in-hand out of the funeral home. He waved goodbye to Gary and me.

I breathed deeply and entered the chapel to remind myself there were no tubes, no anguish, no shots, no more pitiful cries to ever come from my son. He was in heaven. Even though I had accepted errors, I had done the best I could. So had Gary. We thanked God for the peace we saw.

That Tuesday in December, Keith's casket was closed before the afternoon service. It was not re-opened. Keith was home. We placed the boys' remains deeply in the ground at the foot of his grandfather. There was the knowledge within us that another son might not live a normal length life. We provided a place near his brother.

There was more remorse. The untimely death of the accident victim was much more painful than the death of the always ill and suffering child. There, in the Garden of Memories, they rested together. In heaven they lived together. We remained.

We three, weary of the sorrow, returned to Jonesboro Tuesday evening. We called Maggie and otherwise prepared for Wednesday routine as usual. We were still alive. Kirk was too.

Kirk couldn't play outside very much because the weather had become cold and damp. Maggie reported to me that one day Kirk had gone into his room. He looked at the spot where the baby bed used to be. "I miss him," he had said to himself.

Maggie helped Kirk make a fort with quilts over chairs in the living room. Between colds and illnesses various children from the village came to play with him. Often he was invited to visit other children.

Autumn was a favorite girlfriend. She lived just west of our house. She was about a year younger than Kirk. She had reddish-brown hair and twinkling blue eyes.

Kirk came in from outside. "Autumn can't play today. She has a cold." Kirk said as he pushed the door shut.

"Your nose is red. It is that cold outside?" Maggie asked.

"Yep, and I rode my bicycle two times around the carport before I 'froze out'," he said. He was mimicking a colloquial phrase.

"Do you think Kevin might be able to play or do you want me to play checkers with you?" Maggie asked.

"Would you, Maggie?" Kirk was overjoyed and went after the board and pieces to prepare to play.

"Yep, I will!" she replied in his style.

When I entered the game was almost won. Carefully I placed my artwork to be graded on the other end of the kitchen table. "Well Maggie, who is winning?" I asked laughingly.

"Don't ask. Have you been teaching him to play checkers?" she asked in her jolly way.

"No. But, his father has," I replied and continued, "and he beats me too."

Kirk laughed from behind his row of honored kings.

"Kirk, this is Friday. Do you know what that means?" I teased.

"Daddy's ballgame! Do we get to go?" Kirk asked excitedly.

"If you are well and have a nap very soon, we can."

Immediately, Kirk was off the chair and on his way to a short nap.

I went to the chart to determine how his body was doing. "Did Kirk eat well, Maggie?"

"He did. He's been in better spirits since all of Keith's things are gone and the other kids have been able to play with him," she reported.

Keith's passing was harder on him than anything else that has happened," I said softly and intently.

When I called Kirk he was dreaming about the red Farmall tractor. "Mom, I was riding that tractor all over the basketball court!"

"O.K., but now supper is ready." I said hugging my happy child.

We ate alone on game nights. The players ate a planned meal to facilitate their spirit and playing ability. This time to talk was good for both of us. Kirk told me about his play, television programs and things he thought and did. When Gary came home for a rest before going to get dressed and do warm up we were a happy family.

When we went to the field house the teams were already dressed and warming up. Kirk was holding my hand firmly. It took a bit of time for him to get used to the enormous room.

When the excitement and noise of the game got too loud for Kirk he commanded, "Mom, cover my ears!"

I obeyed by placing my fingers over his ears. It blocked much of the sound. Later, I uncovered his ears and asked, "Who's going to hold my ears?"

Kirk laughed and placed my hands firmly against his ears.

I noticed something that hadn't happened before. Kirk was avoiding the excitement of the noise and moved about very little away from me. I wondered, was he weaker than last year, or was it all of the strain of the last few weeks? I tucked the thoughts away. There had been enough sadness, I was just borrowing trouble. I concentrated on the game. Gary was great!

After most of the bleachers had cleared of people, the players' wives and friends took their time to walk down toward the dressing room. We had lots of things in common and found it easy to sit together to give each other support.

"Mom," Kirk pulled my hand, "I want to go get Dad."

"He'll be out in a little while."

"Mom, I want to go now!" Kirk said emphatically.

"Don't get run over by one of the boys. You're little remember that," I warned.

"See you!" he said running toward the door of the dressing room.

The look-alikes were the last ones out of the dressing room. (That was usual.)

"Ready to go home? We're hungry! What's to eat?" Gary asked, fixing Kirk's coat before going out the door of the field house.

"We can have some sandwiches, peaches and cake. How does that sound?" I said securing my own coat belt.

"Good! Let's go Mr. Man!" Gary said gathering his family and feeling good about the game.

The hospital had sent Lola home to her parents' home in Morley. We were relieved. We felt inside that we had begun to live again.

The next weekend Kirk and I decided to get out the ornaments and our silver Christmas tree and to put them together.

"Kirk, be careful with the ornaments. They can get broken very easily," I warned as we decorated our traditional tree.

"Will we have the tree finished when Dad gets home from basketball?" Kirk was wondering.

"I hope so. We have to wrap Daddy's pocketknife. Remember you must not tell him what it is! He won't be surprised if you tell him," I warned.

"I won't. Don't worry, Mom!" Kirk assured emphatically.

Together we placed a brick, some rocks, some stainless steel flatware and some newspaper around the knife in a tennis shoe box. It was taped securely and wrapped in paper from a former Christmas.

"Now, look at that! We did a good job!" I congratulated our work.

"Daddy can shake this one all he wants and he'll never figure it out!" Kirk said remembering his Dad liked to shake presents.

"Yep," I laughed, "we'll fool him this time."

After the accident and Keith's funeral expenses, we had only a small amount of money for presents. The tree didn't have many presents under it.

Kirk continued to think about the tractor, for he spoke of it nearly daily. He knew that money didn't grow on trees. At least that was what he had heard us say. So, because he knew Santa had to be paid for the toys and things, he didn't really expect the tractor to be one of the things Santa would bring him.

Kirk helped gather the presents and clothes for

the brief holiday in Missouri. Gary had only three days off from basketball practice. He had missed enough practices that he didn't want to ask for any more favors.

At Great Grandma and Grandpa's home on Christmas Day, lots of relatives gathered to celebrate. Grandma Lola was still living there with her parents. She had her mouth wired and her arm in a cast from the accident. She was much thinner than before, but happy and pretty as ever. Presents were passed around as was the custom. Kirk loved the excitement. Uncle Den pushed a tractor from the other room into the large living room.

"Kirk, this has your name on it," he advised.

Kirk looked questioningly at the both of us. Was it really for him? We could see his dilemma. He couldn't believe it. He had a sheepish look on his face. Overwhelmed, he began to smile broadly and run to the tractor. He was saying louder and louder as he went, "Oh, goody! OH, GOODY!!"

Lola was near us. When I checked we all three had tears in our eyes.

"Oh Lola," I said with surprise and pleasure, "Thank you."

"Dude would have wanted it this way. He ordered it before the accident."

We watched and visited as the children took turns on the red Farmall tractor. One would pedal and one would ride. Mostly, Kirk rode on the back. He tired easily when he tried to pedal.

As he rode by he called, "Dad, Grandma, I really like the tractor. How did Santa know I'd be here?"

"Grandma must have arranged that," I called back appreciatively.

She looked at me. I said, "He really wanted that. Thank you. You've been very good to us." I was deeply appreciative of her generosity.

"Zoom, zoom," Kirk motorized the tractor as I

peddled through the house. He held on tightly. We laughed when the dust mop almost got us as we went through the hall into Kirk's room.

"When are you going to let me ride on the back while you pedal?" I asked as I puffed from the exercise.

"Oh, Mom, you're too heavy for me!" Kirk laughed. He knew I was kidding.

"See that mop?"

"Yep!" Kirk admitted.

"Well, I have to finish cleaning. So, start pedaling yourself, big man," I said getting off.

He did. Sometimes he found the pedals more difficult to move than others. He pretended to be plowing a field.

"Turn over dirt!" he commanded.

I laughed as I dusted under the couch and called, "There is dirt in here, farmer!"

"Oh, Mom!" he said disgusted with my inability to pretend.

Kirk was weak at times. I began to notice his fatigue more and more. Inside I worried.

Sometimes Gary and I were overcome with the losses. We were regular in our church attendance and I had even been able to practice with the church choir enough to sing in the Christmas Cantata. Kirk had been sitting with Gary in "big church" for the last few weeks. He was good. The children didn't have to be well for him to be in church that way. Kirk knew how to whisper which amused the people around them. Now as I cleaned, I allowed myself to think. I had not allowed thinking, only working for the last month. Inside my spirit I knew God was in control of all things. I didn't understand His ways very well. Just how I could have handled things better in relation to my children was unclear to me. "Oh well," I thought, "At least Kirk is well now." Then I called, "Hey farmer, how about a snack?"

"Yeh, banana!" came the reply followed by my toe-headed, brown-eyed son.

6

Mom, What Is It Like To Die?

Kirk was crying in his sleep. Being roused from sleep by the sound, I went to Kirk's room to his bedside.

"Are you awake?" I asked quietly.

"Mom, I don't want to die like Keif," Kirk said aloud as he continued crying.

I was shocked somewhat. However, my reply came calmly, "You're not going to die now. Someday everybody stops living on the earth." I prayed for calm, strength and wisdom.

"I mean, I don't want to die in the hospital, alone," he sobbed quietly.

I assured him, "You won't, if you don't want to."

I held him in my arms and quieted him. He laid back to sleep as I patted him. Inside I prayed, "Please God, I don't want him to die alone in the hospital either."

Then Kirk sat up. He shook his head as though clearing his mind. I had noticed him doing this more often, lately. He looked into my face and asked, "Mom, what's it like to die? Does it hurt?"

"To die," I began as I summoned all the courage I had, "is like going to sleep and waking up in heaven with Grandpa, Keith and Little Grandma. Best of all, God is there. Jesus loves us very much. No, dying doesn't hurt. When you die you aren't sick or anything." I held this son to my breast and sobbed softly, "I love you. Please try to sleep. Try not to worry."

He laid down again. This time he slept. I didn't.

March winds blew in a cold front. Kirk got chilled and with his weakened heart he developed a fever with a cold. A pneumonia set up the day before Gary was twenty-four years old.

On Wednesday, March 13, 1963 Kirk entered the hospital. This was the second time we had been forced to admit him to the hospital since his diagnosis as cystic fibrosis, three years earlier.

At first the oxygen tent was needed for breathing. Soon they stopped the intravenous solutions because he could take oral medications easily. The pneumonia had begun to subside.

One day as the hospital staff was studying Kirk's case to learn more about cystic fibrosis children, Kirk woke from sleep.

They had gathered around his bed, dressed in white.

Looking at the group in white he said, as he lifted the tent edge, "If I'm dead and in heaven, where are Keif and Grandpa?"

The group was amazed at this young child's faith in life after death. One of the nuns gathered her wits and responded first. "Kirk, you're not in heaven. We are a group of nurses who have come to see you. Are you feeling better?"

"Oh yes, but I'm not all better," he answered politely.

Grandma Lola had come to stay with Kirk during the day while I was teaching and Gary was in school. Kirk liked her to read to him. They enjoyed being

together. Kirk was pleased to have her there especially since he was now able to be out of the tent for
lovin'. (That was what he called being held and
comforted.) He was able to be up for longer periods of
time now.

At school I was working diligently in preparing
the high school ensembles and choir for a Sunday
afternoon concert the first Sunday in April. Gary
was in the midst of mid-term exams. We both found it
difficult to sleep without the compressor running in
the other bedroom.

Kirk was liked in the hospital. His excellent
vocabulary and pleasant personality resulted in the
nurses calling him by name soon after the critical
period was passed. He was confined, but not totally
unhappy. Daily, he told me about what the baby who
was in a bed just outside his door was doing. His
longing for a baby had been temporarily fulfilled.

I prepared to leave for home. It was Friday
evening and nine o'clock. Kirk was two days into the
second week of his stay in the hospital. I told him, "If
you want me, tell the nurse to call me. I'll come as
soon as I can get here. It takes about ten minutes."

"O.K., if I want some lovin', I'll have the nurse
call," he agreed lying down under the tent to sleep.

"The doctor said you might be able to watch a
cartoon tomorrow. So, go to sleep," I concluded
gathering up the rest of my sewing to leave.

"Nurse, please call my Momma. I want some
lovin'," he told the nurse at six-thirty the next
morning.

This nurse hadn't been on duty the night before
and had not been informed of Kirk's way of asking
for attention. She hadn't understood and said, "I'll
check to see if I can call."

Kirk reinforced, "Call her please. I need some lovin'."

Finally, at seven-thirty they did call. He was so upset that they feared a heart attack might occur.

The nurse said, "Kirk has been saying, 'I need some lovin', can you come to the hospital?"

"How long has he been saying it?" I asked hearing my son's near shouts in the background.

"For a while," the nurse said.

"I'll be there in ten minutes. Tell Kirk that," I said indignantly slamming the receiver down in my rush to get to my son. "Kirk has been calling for some lovin'. I'm gone now!" I said emphatically to Gary. I had been washing windows and left one window half washed.

"I'll come later," he assured me.

I ran from the car to the elevator. I was nearly frantic. When the elevator stopped I could hear Kirk. He was shouting.

"I'm here! Hush, hush, Kirk, I'm here," I said gradually quieting my voice. Instantly I had Kirk in my arms and began to pat and stroke his hair. He began to get calmer.

"Why didn't you come? You said you would!" he cried in anguish and relief.

I explained as best I could. I thought as I rocked him, "Hospitals have their place. My son's place is home." I cried as I stroked Kirk's back and rocked him gently in the straight backed chair. Soon, he slept exhausted. I placed him into the oxygen tent as I assured him I would be right here in the chair.

When the doctor came into the room much later, Lola and I were seated beside the bed. Kirk was still sleeping.

Doctor Kemp greeted us sadly, "Kirk is left with only one-fourth of one lung oxygenating his blood. His heart is greatly enlarged, and extremely overworked. At the longest he'll probably not live longer than nine months. I'm very sorry, but those are the facts."

The pain was bad but I looked into the face of the kind, helpful doctor who had seen us through so much. I felt sorry for him too. It must be awful to have to tell people you like this kind of news.

Then I spoke, "I want to take Kirk home, today."

"You may," he consented, "because you know how to care for him."

Lola left to get Gary so they could check Kirk out of the hospital and take care of the bill.

Kirk was going home.

After Kirk woke he said, "Can I watch a cartoon?"

We were walking toward the game room when Kirk grabbed my face and pinched it painfully.

"Stop that, Kirk!" I said smacking him on the leg.

Kirk grimmaced and writhed in pain. I didn't smack him that hard I thought.

Doctor Kemp was watching. He commanded, "There will be no cartoons. Take him back to bed. Put him in the tent."

They increased the oxygen. In a little while he was better. That was the first mild heart attack. I didn't know then what had happened. I just obeyed.

About two-thirty the four of us left the hospital. When we arrived home Kirk went gladly to his own bed. He slept.

We prepared dinner.

I went in to check on Kirk. He was having difficulty in breathing. His speech was slurred.

"Want to watch T.V., Mom," Kirk said weakly.

Kirk indicated he wanted to walk to the living room. He wasn't strong enough so I held him up and allowed him to take a few more steps to the living room. I helped him lay down on the couch.

"Myrna, can't you see he's not strong enough?" Lola said advising me.

I could see. I determined not to tell my son no to

anything else whether he died today or tomorrow. There were no words to express the feeling of despair in my heart. My son was dying and there was no desire to see him suffer anymore. Why should I forbid him to do what he desired now?

He looked toward his father who was near tears and said, "Need my medicine," in the same slurred speech.

I fought back the tears and went to the kitchen to continue with the supper.

The medication was given.

Lola was weeping in the living room. I was in the kitchen. Gary was beside Kirk. We decided to call the doctor.

Kirk stopped breathing. Gary began giving mouth to mouth resuscitation.

I called the doctor when Kirk had first laid down. When I reached him I told him of Kirk's condition. At the time I ended the second sentence Gary told me he had stopped breathing.

The doctor was at the house a few minutes before the ambulance arrived.

The siren of the ambulance alerted the campus. As the sun was setting March 25, 1963 Kirk was pronounced dead. A group of students were standing silently, watching through the door as the end of life arrived. Some were curious, others were sharing in our grief. How could they help but wonder how the three of us who had now lost three loved ones inside of four months could cope with it.

There were no tears in me, only deep sadness. Kirk had departed from illness, loneliness and pain. He wasn't hurting anymore. I hadn't wanted to stop death. I was tired. Emotionally, physically and mentally worn to near the breaking point. The Lord would give me the grace to cope. I knew that.

We had no fear of death. Living was much more difficult. Gary wept openly. Lola was lamenting three not one.

I turned to the technicians and the doctor and said, "Thank you, you did all there was to do. Please (I motioned to Gary) Gary needs some time."

The ambulance men waited before taking the body. Our friend, Dean Moore comforted Gary. I looked back to Kirk's body. There wasn't any movement, nor life. Yet, inside me there was a sensing that he was still there asking what to do next. I didn't see anything or hear with my ears, but if he was asking, I'd better answer. Even now, he was still my son, why shouldn't I answer. I thought, "It's all right. We'll be O.K. It's time for you to go to heaven. Goodbye. Tell Keith I love him. I love you. Goodbye, dear son. Go!"

What adventures he'll have to tell us someday, I thought. Then I cried too.

The funeral was Monday. We returned to classes on Wednesday. Now we cried to sleep in each others arms often. Gary was having a harder time with the grief than I was. I was just plain lonesome. We made plans for me to go back to college to finish my degrees.

The Sunday concert was a success. The audience was so subdued that after my solo "Getting to Know You" there was no applauding at first, then the rafters rang. Later I realized that they were thinking about the things that had happened to me during the year of teaching. Earlier they had given me a corsage they had made out of money. When the teachers had given it to me, I at first, hadn't noticed the creation was of money. The students and teachers had had a benefit game at school to raise money for us. I had been overwhelmed at their generosity. Now the applauding made more sense. They were saying we love you. We're with you. "As a teacher I've been learning, you'll forgive me if I boast, but I've become an expert on the subject I like most, getting to know you..." had been words which pricked their very hearts. No wonder their reaction didn't dawn on me at first. I was responsible for a program and wasn't thinking about me at all. That's how I lived for the next years. Never, did I think about me. There was husband, home and work to think about. I didn't mourn nor allow self-pity! I received congratulations for the students singing joyfully. They had been great. The final song, "Were you there?" had been a double-chorus work. It was magnificent! We celebrated the excellence of their concert together. I had begun to live again!

Gary Kirk at
age 15 months.
November 1960.

Sons Keith and
Kirk. Picture
was taken
Fall of 1962.

Myrna, Keith and Kirk at home in Jonesboro, Arkansas, Fall 1962.

Sons Keith and Kirk. Picture was taken Fall of 1962 at home in Jonesboro following the command "Hush Kief!".

Epilogue

Epilogue

"What has happened in the twenty years since this experience?" you ask.

Are you to ready to receive the shock twenty years have brought?

After my sons died, my career bloomed. My pride caused sin to creep in. Though I faithfully tithed and worked many hours for the church, my personal life was scarred and finally there was divorce. When all my strength was gone, and my endurance was gone, God provided a way. He sent me His example and word of His power through a friend. Late in 1972, He sent me His comforter. I was home alone with God. My sins were confessed and my heart right with God when Jesus baptized me with the power sent from the Father.

> "When the Comforter is come, whom I will send unto you from the Father, even the Spirit of truth, which proceedeth from the Father, he shall testify of me. (John 15:26)
>
> "... he shall baptize you with the Holy Spirit and with fire." (Luke 3:16)

Spiritual growth as never before began in me.

> "But the Comforter, which is the Holy Ghost, whom the Father will send in my name, he shall teach you all things, and bring all things to your remembrance, whatsoever I have said unto you." (John 14:26)

Trials were rough. In 1978 I resigned from teaching (after 18 years) at the gentle prompting of the Lord. Finally, I was mentally dead to myself!

> "I am crucified with Christ; nevertheless I live; yet not I but Christ liveth in me; and the life which I now live in the flesh I live by the faith of the Son of God, who loved me, and gave himself for me." (Galatians 2:20)

The necessity for confession of sins daily caused me to know the truth of the scriptures.

> "If we confess our sins, he is faithful and just to forgive us our sins, and cleanse us from all unrighteousness." (I John 1:9)

My days began early with praise to God. Prayer and joy grew within me. God began showing me why my sons died. The symptoms of cystic fibrosis were evident within my own body. I sought the Lord for answers to the questions in my mind. He began teaching me.

> "Thou shalt not bow down thyself to them, nor serve them: for I the Lord thy God am a jealous God, visiting the iniquity of the fathers upon the children unto the third and fourth generation of them that hate me. And showing mercy unto thousands of them that love me and keep my commandments." (Exodus 20:5-6)
>
> "A bastard (child resulting from prohibited marriages) shall not enter into the congregation of the Lord. An Ammonite or Moabite shall not enter into the congregation of the Lord; even to their tenth generation shall they not enter into the congregation of the Lord forever . . . (Of Edomites) The children that are begotten of them shall enter into the congregation of the Lord in their third generation." (Dueteronomy 23:2-3, 8)

My thankfulness grew and grew as he taught me of the provisions the Father had made for me and others who were genetically ill. That was why Jesus had to die on a cross. No other death would free us from the iniquities of the fathers (ancestral line)!

> "And the goat shall bear upon him all their iniquities unto a land not inhabited; and he shall let go the goat in the wilderness." (Leviticus 16:22)
>
> "If a man have committed sin worthy of death, and he be to be put to death, and thou hang him of a tree; (crucify) his body shall not remain all night upon the tree, but thou shalt in any wise bury him that day; (for he that is hanged is ACCURSED OF GOD); that thy land be not defiled, which the Lord thy God giveth thee for an inheritance." (Deuteronomy 21:22-23)
>
> "Christ hath redeemed us from the curse of the law, being made a curse for us; for it is written, Cursed is every one that hangeth on a tree: That the blessings of Abraham might come on the Gentiles through Jesus Christ; that we might receive the promise of the Spirit through faith." (Galatians 3:13-14)

After a severe illness and offering up what was left of my life to the Lord I asked for the Lord Jesus to "Make my pancreas work, please, because of your mercy." The pancreatic reconstruction was so gradual that only after it was completed did I become aware God had given what I had asked! The accompanying "chronic bronchitis" which had always bothered me had also improved dramatically. I was still unable to memorize or play any music which required left-right coordination. My dyslexia (a learning disability) was the same though I had asked the Lord to heal it. Something was still missing waiting for me to search and discover the hidden truth.

> "Think not that I come to destroy the law, or the prophets; I am not come to destroy but to fulfill. For verily I say unto you till heaven and earth pass, one jot or one tittle shall in no wise pass from the law, till all be fulfilled." (Matthew 5:17-18)

Diligently I began to search again the things which God said would bring changed conditions (curses) in Deuteronomy 27 and 28.

" . . . The Lord will make thy plagues wonderful (tragic), and the plagues of thy seed, even great plagues, and of long continuance, and sore sicknesses, and of long continuance. . . " (Deuteronomy 28:58-60)

Jesus paid the perfect redemptive cost for my freedom and my sons on the cross.

"O.K., you mean that had you declared your sons free they probably would have lived and been alive today?" you ask wanting to understand.

Yes, my ignorance of the Bible and God's perfect plan for freedom allowed Satan to steal my sons! Believe me, many hours were spent in deep remorse and grief for this truth.

"What happened when you began seeing this truth?" you probe.

Amid tears I began this book. That was five years ago. Also, when the first draft was finished I went to the Lord and asked for his mercy to let me start over again. My life was of no value to me unless God had something for me to do for Him. I recommitted my life to him. At twelve years of age I had gone forward in a Billy Graham meeting to dedicate my life for total use of God. The call was to be a teacher to the body of Christ. I didn't understand the call at twelve, but at forty I did. My old self was not completely dead! The mourning for my sons was opening me to a different type of attack. Emotionally, though I had asked to start over I was obsessed with thoughts of dying. The Lord sent a long-time friend who saw the problem and helped rid my mind of these awful torments.

"That ye put off concerning the former conversation the old man, which is corrupt according to the deceitful lusts: And be renewed in the spirit of your mind: And that ye put on the new man,which after God is created in righteousness and true holiness." (Ephesians 4:22-24)

"How much more shall the blood of Christ, who through the eternal Spirit offered him without spot to God, purge your conscience from dead works to serve the living God?" (Hebrews 9:14)

As Ezekiel announced, God needs thousands to pray for others. Many hours were spent in prayer for others. As the Lord called, I was faithful to spend hours in prayer. As I prayed for people, I grew to love them as the Father had loved me. *Agape*, the God-kind of love, was now my motivational force. God continued to pull on my heart toward formal full-time work for him. I didn't see a way, but God was in charge.

The Loving Mercy of God

The return to His way started when I was in the Post Office in Sikeston, Missouri on January 15, 1979.

On that crisp January morning, the Lord caused me to meet a pastor friend of long years casual acquaintance.

His wife of thirty-three years had died of accute septicemia two months previous to our meeting. He had been crying. His face was swollen because of the tears.

I went to him because of Christian compassion, "How are you, Brother Grady?" I asked gently, "How are you, really?"

His reply shocked me, "I'm awful! I never understood about the loss of a mate until it happened to me. And today Marie's sister is being operated on for possible cancer. My daughter is unable to go anywhere alone. I'm terrible!"

"I know preachers can't talk to everybody. We've lost a sister, Margie. Mom and Dad are close-mouthed, understanding people. Why don't you go to talk to them."

In my mind I had no design on him. He was a Baptist preacher. They didn't approve of divorce. I spoke with other tongues and they certainly didn't "cotton" to that! He's almost as old as my Mom—so I thought they would be able to help him.

"Okay I might," Grady said as we walked out of the Post Office into the parking lot.

"I'll pray for you." I said.

He answered, "I will!"

I thought aloud softly, "And Lord, he can't hear either!"

June thirtieth after an upsetting day we were married at Mom and Dad's trailer at 6:00 P.M. The beige dress bought a year earlier, but never worn, was my wedding dress. God let me start over with a man who loved Him, spoke in other tongues and believed divorce was a sin forgiveable under I John 1:9 like all other sins. What was in my heart at that time? *"A ehm' a ha!"* Later Grady gave me the interpretation, "How great is the mercy of God!"

An evangelist moving mightily in gifts of the Holy Spirit came to Sikeston for a meeting starting November 16, 1979. I knew I was to go, though we were pastoring a Baptist Church. Inside I sensed it was my time to get something special from the Lord. Maybe it was my time to be free of the rest of my hereditary diseases, dyslexia. I had been seeking and learning of scriptures on the "iniquities of the fathers to the third and fourth generation." I earnestly desired to be able to play the piano without that handicap. The righteousness of Jesus grew strong in me.

"The eyes of the Lord are over the righteous, and his ears are open unto their prayers (I Peter 3:12)

At the meeting Alfred Hinton prayed for several people before he pointed me out. We had never met.

He knew nothing of my problems. Like Elisha, he had been given his knowledge from the Lord. He spoke through the knowledge of God's Holy Spirit.

"Yes, Ma'am, Lady, you've been ordained to walk in the spirit. God's made a spiritual woman of you. You haven't understood the strangeness of your life. You've wondered about it, because you were so different."

"You have this nerve—problem in your vision. I'm seeing your left vision—here needs to be strengthened by the Lord. It would be your left—to me it's your right. But it's your left facing like this. Huh? It's gonna be healed. Jesus is gonna make you well."

"The Lord has called you to do a work for Him. Better than three to four years ago there was a "voice" given to pump you. That's right the Lord pumps on your heart of faith. But trials came up and the Devil tried to make pieces of you, but he couldn't do it."

"That's right!!"

"I also see the Devil has used loved ones to war on you to tear you apart. I see a family separation has torn you."

"That's right!"

"But, God is going to intervene for you, and you are going to see something. The Lord's love will flow among your kin people like you desire. There's a sister figure for which your heart has been much broken."

"That's right!"

"She has not understood your work for God. I believe she has formed things wrong. You've been hurt because of her misconception of you, but you keep standing true to God and God will prove all things. Don't try to prove anything yourself. You just remain where the Lord wants you and God will exalt you in your season."

I cried softly. I expected something unusual to heat my body or shake me or something else different.

Yet, inside I received my reconstruction by faith. My reconstructive miracle was without evidence! None! Nothing! "Strange, but though nothing has happened to my head—I know that I'm healed!" I told Grady. We were on the way home to our comfortable, modest home God has allowed us to purchase.

"Well, just keep on believing. God wouldn't say that if He weren't going to do something good!" he comforted wisely.

When we prayed together, Grady thanked God for fixing my dyslexia and reminded God that He does all things well.

His words were true. All night long the feeling of static electricity worked through my body. I slept intermittently as the Lord rewired my nervous system part of the way. Many other times the Lord has worked on my central nervous system to go on with the reconstruction of more of the nerves as I was more obedient, and as I could adjust to the radical changes in my ability to see things as they are. I fell out the back door one time because the step was where I saw it instead of where it used to be before my vision was fixed. The Lord deals with us in His perfect justice and will for our own good.

In the morning my head was a different shape. I went to the piano to try playing a Bach two-part Invention. I could play it slowly for the first time in my life. I fell over a chair on the way to fix breakfast. I missed my fork on the first try. My eyes were definitely different! I said to the Lord as I put in a load of laundry, "Lord, what's going on? I'm falling over everything. Everything seems a bit different."

Grady came to breakfast. When the washer got to the end of the cycle the clutch let out it's usual long high-pitched wail.

"Boy, what's wrong with that washing machine? I've never heard that noise before!" Grady said emphatically.

"That's the one"—I stopped short, "Honey, your ears have been healed! Praise God, we've both got our miracles!"

We celebrated together in a tearful round of laughter and praise to God!

The process of learning that everything you see, is where you see it and not moving about, is some experience! All my forty-one years of compensation were being reversed. It was not all at once, but enough so I could tell the difference! My rewiring work was continued periodically by the Holy Spirit, usually at night.

I put my prism glasses aside. I could see better without them than with them.

"Well, finally I'm seeing some progress in your nervous system!" the doctor said to me on the Monday following the Friday evening meeting.

"Praise God!" I said.

A week later I told the whole story.

I thanked him for the two years of help. I haven't returned for further treatment.

Grady and I continued growing in skill in yielding to be used of the Holy Spirit. We began ministering by the power of the Lord to others.

Grady's daughter became able to work and live alone in her own apartment in California. She is no longer agoraphobic! She is married and has established a home of her own.

We are no longer two separate people. We are one flesh. God has put us together. Men will not separate us. (Matthew 19:6)

I continue reminding myself that the Lord will work all things out which concern my life. He said He would. (Psalm 138:8) Always I am acutely aware to thank God for His mercy.

"God really does let people start over?" you ask unbelieving, yet realizing God never gives up on anyone seeking to be near Him.

"Yes, bless His Holy name, He does!"

"How did all this affect your Bible study on genetic diseases?" you ask.

"Up to this time in my mind the real "key" to unlock genetic diseases wasn't complete. I understood what Hosea 4:6 meant when Hosea penned "my people perish for lack of knowledge . . . " When we omit God from our lives, He said He would forget us!"

Why We Are Ill

"The Bible says in Micah 6:13 and Isaiah 33:24 that when there is sin there will be illness. Satan uses every opportunity to kill or disable God's children. He also kills his own to prevent them from believing. During a weekly Bible study my two students and I began searching for indicators stating why people were sick. We found they were ill for one of six reasons (The number six refers to "man," (i.e.), God's dealing with man. A complete study on Biblical Reasons For Illness" is available on cassette.)

The Bible showed we were ill because: 1) We are guilty of sins. God allows us to be afflicted. 2) Our ancestors were guilty of sins for which they never repented. God allowed their children to be afflicted to the 3rd or 4th generation. There were numerous accounts in the Bible using both sin forms as the cause for illnesses. 3) We were tested and tried to demonstrate our love and obedience to God. There were numerous references to this reason for persecution and some illness. (I Peter 1:6-7) 4) We were ill due to poor dietary habits, lack of rest, or eating blood. (Acts 15:29) There were many citations to this as well as to the effects of old age. 5) We were blind, or died and raised from the dead to give glory to the Lord Jesus. There were six instances in the New Testament and three in the Old Testament. 6) Three were left with an infirmity of body to remind them of their meeting and covenant with the Lord. (Jacob, Moses, Paul)."

"Genetic illness is the second group? Why did God do that?" you ask honestly.

"Please be patient. This is a long answer. I pray it is your key to wholeness."

Why God Allows Genetic Diseases

Because God never changes (Hebrews 13:8) He will allow what He has said will occur. He said He would visit the sins of the parents on their children to the third and fourth generations, or to the tenth in some instances of sins, (Dueteronomy chapters 23, 27 and 28). With each pronouncement of judgement God sent a means of mercy. He sent Jesus, the perfect blend of sacrifice and judgment. "When we confess our sins, He is faithful and just to forgive us our sins and to cleanse us from all unrighteousness." (I John 1:9) The confession of sins was one of the things I was to search the scriptures to document.

During six months I read the Bible entirely. A cross reference of the scriptures on 1) iniquities of the fathers; 2) death of sons, children or seed; and 3) why we are ill, was completed. God is bound to His word. He doesn't change! He said certain sins would cause changed conditions or "curses" to become part of a child's inheritance.

I questioned. What had I inherited as a consequence of my forefathers spiritual accounts? What had I inherited genetically? What physically? In what ways did I mimic their attitudes and habits? Was I a Balaam? Was I a cursed child? (II Peter 2:14-15) My account was a mess. I went back to self-examination and confession!

As I studied further I learned of Nehemiah 9:2. All Israel read the law one fourth of the day. Next they confessed their sins and the sins of their fathers for the next fourth of the day. They sat before the Lord humbled and with fasting.

Our God of Confession

I imagined I was there for the same week of time before the Lord. They had been away from Jerusalem (God's city) and Jehovah. They had borne the effects of their fathers' sin. I realized my position before the Lord was essentially the same. My fasting now included the provision of Nehemiah 9:2-3. I confessed the sins of my ancestors. This will not change their eternal standing before Jehovah God! Ezekiel 18 clearly and repeatedly states my eternal relationship to Him is my choice. So it was my ancestor's choice to serve or not to serve the living God. What I was seeking was absolution from the effects of their sins.

With self-searching and the "do nots" of the law to guide me, my confession continued. God's prompting may require you to put feet and actions to the confessions. Secret resentments, unforgiveness and sins had to go! Attitudes and acts of a believer must clearly reflect faith, gentleness, meekness, long suffering, goodness and temperance. (Galatians 5:22) (II Kings 7:40-41) (II Chron. 30:7-9) (Mark 11:26)

For me to claim God's provisions I had to stand spiritually where He could bless me. I was cleansing my hands and heart. My mind was being renewed by God's word, the Bible. I was humbled before God. God could draw near to me, as He had always desired.

Draw Near and Stay Near

For two years I had requested a nervous system which could remember music and work normally. Jesus did it! The Father said through Isaiah 57:19 that "He creates the fruit of the lips for His children who are near." When I drew near He "fixed" my nervous system so much in one night that it was obvious to me that God had touched me.

Praise Daily and Testify of God's Mercy

From that day to now each day I praise God for the reconstructive, recreative miracle of vision and normal nervous system function. On the inside all my systems may still be abnormal. I don't know. It is not important. My eyes work normally as does my nervous system. Each day I praise my Lord, God and Creator. He created me to praise Him. Only someone "alive to God" can praise Him. In the reality of praise toward our Lord Jesus the Christ we become truly alive to God's omniscient presence within our being. (Psalm 22:3) Being dead to ourself (Galatians 2:20) and alive to God we are able to walk in love, and in health. (Ephesians 5:1-20)

Satan Had a Legal Right

Remember, the genetic disease was there because of sin. As a result, Satan had a legal right to afflict us. God allowed our ancestor's sins to be visited upon us. Only God's intervention could change this visitation. What Satan did he had an okay from God to do. (Isaiah 54:16 and John 10:10)

In some families an ancestor's condition is accepted as an unfortunate "cross to bear." A Christian should not stop seeking God until the reason for the sickness (See the six reasons for illness) is determined before God by fasting, confession and prayer. Don't bear "crosses" without entreating the Lord! Paul did three times. He sought to undo the effects of his encounter with God. God said, "My grace is sufficient." Paul understood that he tended to be proud. His eye problem was a constant reminder of his encounter with Y'shua! (Acts 9:1-20; II Cor. 12:1-12;

Gal. 4:13-15) Never again does the Bible say he sought God to remove that infirmity of his eyes.

A genetic infirmity has a totally different origin from Paul's problem. The scripture shows the eternal one of Israel provided the way to wholeness. There is freedom from genetic illnesses.

Y'shua (Jesus) Crucified for the Genetically Ill

Y'shua, Messiah, King Eternal, Almighty God, Lord, God of the Universe, the Lily of the Valley, Counselor, Wonderful, The Mighty God, The Holy One of Israel, God Incarnate, God with us paid for our wholeness by being crucified. Jesus, the Christ, truly provided the perfect sacrifice. The provisions were His stripes for healing. Healing is translated from a word which means whatever was needed to make us well physically and spiritually. Isaiah 53:4-5 lists four great benefits Jesus earned to free us from the effects of the sin nature. The words used are griefs, sorrows, transgressions and iniquities.

The death of a child is an immeasurable loss. God understood that. He told us that children are a blessing from Him. (Psalm 127:3) God requested His Son to become limited to the form of a man. He further planned a secret plan to request His only Son to die the death of a criminal. Deuteronomy 21:23 stated that anyone crucified became accursed of God. Jesus agreed to that for us. God himself bore our punishment. He offered up His only Son. He called Jesus, "His gift to men." The genetically ill (cursed) children of men who accept Jesus were freed and restored when the nails were driven through Jesus' hands and feet! Jesus was lifted aloft to die (Galatians 3:13) and set us free from the curse! The plan was in the mind of the Father from before the fall of the first Adam! (I Cor. 2:7-14a)

Jesus' blood was taken to heaven to eternally cover our sins. By faith we ask Jesus (Y'shua) to cover our sins with His blood and give us His righteousness before the Father. (John 3:16) We didn't deserve such love from the heart of God, but we humbly apply it to our sin stained lives. Jesus is our Lord! He is our savior! His name is given to us to be used in our battles with the enemy of God. (Phil. 2:1-15; Matt. 28:18; James 4:7; Mark 16:15-20) Only by the power of Jesus' mighty name are we victorious.

Unlocking Genetic Disease

1. Become obedient, broken and humble before the Lord. Pray and seek the Healer, not the healing. Seek to live for the Lord. (Matt. 6:33) Fast, (Isaiah 58:6) and confess your sins and the sins of your fathers'. Confess what sins you know about. (Nehemiah 9:2) Become able to die to yourself and to be alive to God's leading. (Gal. 2:20)
2. Confess that Jesus has paid the price for your freedom from genetic diseases on the cross. Praise God aloud that you are free as are your children through the tenth generation from genetic diseases. Aloud tell satan that you know your rights as a Christian. (I assume that you have confessed Jesus as your Lord and Savior.) (Daniel 9:3-11; Nehemiah 8:18-9:3) Continue into praises.
3. Ask for a creative, restorative or recreation miracle. Pray and let God lead you as to what to ask for. Jesus said, "Ask anything in My name and I'll do it." (John 14:13-18) "We know we have anything we ask that is God's will." (I John 5:14-15) Because of the death of Jesus on the cross we know wholeness from genetic disease is God's will.

To further point this out, consider the woman with the chronic issue of blood. It was costly and defiling. She was made whole of her plague immediately! (Mark 5:33-34) She testified to others.

In contrast, the blind young man was the subject of the disciples' conversation. Jesus' answer pointed out the nature of this man's problem was not iniquities of his parents nor himself. He was born blind so God might be glorified. (John 9:1-3) Notice he was not in pain, nor did the condition totally interfere with his life. He was totally restored by the obedient, ritualistic washing away of the mud and spittal by the water at the Word of God. At once the young man gave a simple, definitive, factual description of the miracle. "I was blind and now I see."

4. Expect a gradual reversal of symptoms if the change is not immediate. Praise God daily for Jesus' perfect sacrifice. Because of it, you, your household and those you pray for are strengthened and continue to be made whole by the power of Jesus' name and the work of the Holy Spirit. Praise God for what He continues to do. (Stay close to God. Determine to be obedient to the teachings of the scriptures. Daily Bible study is imperative and builds your faith, as you determine to trust and act on the Words of God.) As an intercessor, purge your life before God with self-denial and Bible study to assure powerful use by the Father. (Matthew 17:14-21) Included is a suggested prayer. Ask God for specific prayer details.

When you become discouraged think of what happened to my sons because I didn't follow God's directions. Please, for Jesus' sake, don't ignore God's directions. Be wise, use the provision Jesus perfected for breaking genetic diseases.

Sample Prayer

Breaking and Repairing the
Effects of Genetic Diseases (Affirmation)

Lord Jesus Christ, I believe you died on the cross for my sins and rose again from the dead. You redeemed me and my family by the mode of your death, crucifixion, from the curse of the law. You redeemed me/us from the effects of our sins by the blood of your sacrifice and from all sickness by your stripes.

I belong to you, and I want to live for you (Matt. 16:24-25). I confess all my sins, known and unknown (I John 1:9). I'm sorry for them all. I renounce them all. I forgive all others as I want to be forgiven by you. Forgive me now and cleanse me with your blood. I thank you for the blood of Jesus which cleanses me NOW from all sins.

(Plea for freedom)

I come to you now as my deliverer. You know my special needs—the thing(s) that bind(s), that torment(s), that defile(s), that unclean spirit(s)—I claim the promise of your Word, "Whosoever that calleth on the name of the Lord shall be delivered" I call upon you now. In the name of the Lord Jesus Christ we and our children are delivered from genetic defect(s) of _____, _____, _____, etc., and all tissue defects of the _____, _____, etc., systems of our bodies. We call upon you now and declare in Jesus' name we are delivered from all genetic curses imposed upon us by Satan.

(Loosing)

Satan, in the name of Jesus, we renounce you and all your works. We hereby command that you loose and desist from your assignment against our family through the 10th generation in the name of Jesus. (5th - Ex. 20:5; 10th Deut. 23:2) We command you to leave us right now, we command in the mighty name of Jesus! AMEN (so be it!)

(Pause in the prayer)

(Do as you are directed by the Holy Spirit. Pray, praise and read scriptures until the manifestation of deliverance is spiritually or physically discerned and evident—or as you are led by the Holy Spirit.

(Pause)

The Spirit may quicken you to call out specific spirits. Be open to His leading. PRAISE IS OF THE UTMOST IMPORTANCE in breaking the controls that have been over a family for many generations.)
(Thanksgiving and Praise)
Father God, we thank you for your son, Jesus. We praise you that He has given us HIS POWER over all infirmity, illness, lameness, blindness, deafness, maimness in Jesus' name.
(Healing, recreation and restoration)
We thank you now for normal _____, _____, etc., tissue(s) being healed, recreated or created. We praise you for ___(person's name)___, restoration, recreation, creation and healing.
Praises to you Jesus! You are our creator, restorer, recreator and our healer! ALL HAIL KING JESUS!

Effects of Prayer

For five years I've witnessed change after change in others who have been touched by the master, Jesus. Don't accept Satan's work as the natural course of things. Force yourself to see a whole child in your arms. Rejoice that God is able to both create and remake. Do this daily until you know deep within yourself that God wants you to have whole children. Pray so that God can begin to answer your request.

My own family had many problems (curses) and God allowed me to start there. My own experience led quickly to application of the simple truth to my sister's barrenness. She's mother to two. My #1 nephew is normal in size and not C.F. My #3 nephew is normal mentally and is not hydrocephalic. (A sonagram showed abnormal head size in the 8th month of development.) My #2 nephew developed a rare, sex-linked type (usually cancerous) tumor at the base of the skull. My mother and I agreed that no more sons would be stolen by Satan. His tumor was empty. He's well and normal.

My fasting and praying enlarged to friends. God corrected: psoriasis, Bell's palsy, incorrectly formed heart (It went back to normal before the operating doctor's eyes.), abnormally large tonsils and adenoids, kidney function (genetic), learning disability (severe dyslexia), color blindness, abnormal male body system, crossed eyes, club feet, blood disease, multiple birth defects (heart, hip joint, leg lengthened, etc.), vitiligo, and by faith your problem too. Some were obvious miracles. Other changes were gradual. GOD WORKS HIS WAYS. DON'T LIMIT GOD.

Several persons who have been helped by this God provided way are willing to counsel with you. Their names are listed below. Seek the Lord before you get in contact with one of us. He may send you to someone close by.

Teaching is my calling. Should your group desire teaching please contact me at the following address for our ministry. My husband is called as an apostle to the body of Christ. He edifies churches.

Myrna L. Etheridge of G & M Etheridge Ministries, Inc.
P.O. Box 564
Sikeston, Missouri 63801
Phone (314) 471-9344

Rev. David and Harriet Craig of Craig Ministries, Inc.
Route 1
Essex, Missouri 63846
Phone (314) 283-5673

Jennifer Lee (niece) foreground, L. to R. "Donnie" (nephew), Myrna, "Chris" (nephew). September 1982.

Photo by John Smelcer © 1984

Grady L. Etheridge, Pastor, 1st So. Baptist Church, Lakewood, California. February 1984.

Myrna and Grady Etheridge after church February 5, 1984 in Lakewood, California.

Appendix I

Suggested Readings

Collingraide, Ruth and Jo Ann Sekowsky. *Introduction to Priase. Workshop Series No. W1.* Lynwood, Washington: Women's Aglow Fellowship, 1981

Kuhlman, Kathryn, *Nothing is Impossible With God.* New York: Pillar Books, 1976

Lindsay, Gordon (ed.). Scenes Beyond the Grave, Visions of Marietta Davis. 1885. (33rd ed., 1978) Dallas, Texas: Christ for the Nations, Inc., 1978 reprint.

Thompson, Ann, *What Happened to Bethany?* New York: Tyndale House Publishers, Inc., 1972

Appendix II

Scripture Reference Lists

Any scripture (not out of context) that fits your need, or **ANY SCRIPTURE GOD MAKES COME ALIVE to you** may be used to fight any attack of the enemy.

NOTE - This list is not exhaustive for any single subject other than the scriptures dealing with the iniquities of the fathers to the seed. To the best of my knowledge the iniquities of the fathers scriptures are complete for those scriptures relative to the subject of this study, CURSES AND THE INIQUITIES OF THE FATHERS TO THE SONS AND THE CONFESSION OF THEM.

May you grow as much in the learning of these scriptures for yourself as I grew in the gathering of them for this study.

CHARACTER OF GOD
Exodus 34:5-7
II Chronicles 19:7

SURETY OF JUDGEMENT
Nahum 1:23, 8
Psalm 89:30-34
Ecclesiastes 12:13-14
Hebrews 9:27

SURETY OF JUDGEMENT *continued*
    Hebrews 10:12-39
    Ezekiel 33:12-20
    Ezekiel 17:18-19
    Ezekiel 18:
    Ezekiel 28:18
    Ezekiel 32:27-28
    Amos 3:2
    Jeremiah 5:25
    Isaiah 59:2

INTEGRITY OF GOD'S HOLY BIBLE
    Hebrews 6:13-20
    II Timothy 3:16
    Psalm 19:9-10
    Psalm 12:6
    Psalm 33:4
    Psalm 102:18-21
    Numbers 23:19
    I Samuel 15:29
    Psalm 138:2
    Psalm 119:140-142
    John 17:17
    Ephesians 1:13
    Isaiah 55:8-13
    Galatians 3:23-29
    Matthew 5:17-20
    Luke 16:16-17
    Romans 13:8-10

BIBLE BUILDS FAITH
    Romans 10:17
    Mark 11:22

BIBLE USES TWO WITNESSES
  AND HOPE
    Deut. 17:6
    Matthew 18:16

BIBLE USES TWO WITNESSES
AND HOPE *continued*
John 8:17-18
II Corinthians 13:1
Hebrews 10:28-39

ASK GOD FOR MERCY
Isaiah 55:6-7
Daniel 9:9
II Chronicles 30:9b
Exodus 20:5-6
James 5:11
Hebrews 4:16
Psalm 41:8-10 (especially 10)
Psalm 86
Psalm 89:1-2
Psalm 101:1
Psalm 103:9-11
Psalm 106:43-48
Psalm 117:1-2
Psalm 130:1-8 (especially 3,4)
Psalm 136
I John 3:21-24
Daniel 4:27
Psalm 33:22

OUR GOD OF CONFESSION
Matthew 12:36-37
Proverbs 12:17-19
Isaiah 57:19
Isaiah 8:20
Romans 10:9-10
Jeremiah 23:36
Psalm 77:12
Proverbs 13:2-3
Luke 6:43-45

NATURE AND STATE AND STANDING OF MAN

STATE
Romans 3:23
Psalm 58:3
Psalm 55:8

STANDING
Ezekiel 18:entire, (4,20)
Ezekiel 33:12-30
Deut. 24:16
Romans 6:23
Romans 10:9-10
John 1:12
II Kings 14:5-6
II Chronicles 6:23, 32-36
II Chronicles 34:24,25; 27-28, 31-33
II Chronicles 25:4
Jeremiah 31:30
Titus 3:5
Psalm 90:7-8
Isaiah 59:2-13
Isaiah 64:7
Joshua 24:15b

SEEING OURSELVES AS GOD DOES
Job 42:1-6
Psalm 51:11-13
Ezekiel 36:31-33
Ezekiel 43:10
Isaiah 64:4-9
Psalm 8:4-9
Psalm 90:7-8

RESULT OF SEEING OURSELVES AS GOD DOES
Galatians 2:20
John 3:16

RESULT OF SEEING OURSELVES AS GOD DOES *continued*
Galatians 4:1-7
Hebrews 9:14
Titus 3:5
Romans 12
I John 3:1-24 (especially 22)
Ezekiel 36:24-27
Matthew 28:19-20
Mark 16:15-20
James 5:16
I Corinthians 7:20-24
Luke 14:11

GOD FIGHTS OUR BATTLES
II Chronicles 20:15b
II Chronicles 32:7-8
I Samuel 17:47
Psalm 23:1

REMITTING THE SIN OF ANOTHER PERSON
John 20:23
II Corinthians 2:10
Acts 7:60

BREAKING BONDAGE BY FASTING
Isaiah 58:6-14
Mark 9:29
Luke 11:8-26
Matthew 12:22-45; 17:21
Luke 10:37-42
John 14:12
Romans 8:26-28

JESUS, GOD'S PROVISION FOR TAKING OUR SINS
Galatians 3:13
Deut. 21:22-23

JESUS, GOD'S PROVISION
FOR TAKING OUR SINS *Continued*
John 3:14
John 12:32
Isaiah 53:11
Col. 2:14

PRAYER: THANKING AND ASKING THE
FATHER FOR HELP IN JESUS' NAME
Psalm 50:16
James 5:16
Col. 4:2,12
Psalm 17:1
Matthew 18:18-20
John 7:37-38
I John 5:14-15
John 14:12-15; 15:5-7; 11:22
John 16:23-24
Matthew 28:19-20
Jude 20
I Corinthians 14:4,14,15
I Thessalonians 5:17
Ezekiel 9:4-6; 22:30
I Timothy 2:1
Ephesians 6:10-18
Philemons 4:6-7
I Timothy 4:4-5
Ephesians 5:17-20
Romans 8:26-28
Romans 11:2
Isaiah 64:7; 59:16
Jeremiah 7:16
Jeremiah 15:1

REASONS FOR PLAGUES OR CURSES ON SEED
Exodus 20:5
Matthew 5:17
Deut. 27:15-26

REASONS FOR PLAGUES
OR CURSES ON SEED *Continued*

Leviticus 18:6
Deut. 18:9-14
Col. 3:5
Deut. 12:23-25
Acts 15:20,29
Psalm 119:21
Proverbs 6:16-19
Jeremiah 11:3
Jeremiah 17:5
Jeremiah 48:10
Deut. 23:2
II Corinthians 6:14
Numbers 30
Ecc. 5:4-5
Malachi 1:14
Malachi 2:2
Malachi 3:9
Numbers 5:23
Deut. 28:15
Numbers 22:6
Numbers 24:9
Galatians 2:8
Galatians 3:10
Galatians 3:13
Deut. 21:22-23
2 Peter 2:9-14
Deut. 30:19

CONDITIONS RESULTANT FROM
● CHANGED CONDITIONS (CURSES)

Deut. 28:16-end of chapter (50 specific
conditions listed)

RESULT OF SINS

CONFUSION OF MIND

Isaiah 43:24-26 (especially 25)

RESULT OF SINS *Continued*

CONFUSION OF MIND
Hosea 9:7
Psalm 106:14-15
Psalm 135:13-18
Psalm 97:7
Proverbs 5:22-23 (bonds)
Isaiah 63:10

ILLNESS
Isaiah 33:24
Micah 6:13
Lamentations 5:7
Psalm 107:17-20
Psalm 38:3-5, 15
Jeremiah 30:8-17 (accidents)

LACK OF SPIRITUAL BLESSING
Jeremiah 5:23-25
Psalm 106:13-15

GETTING RID OF FEAR
Isaiah 41:10
I John 4:18
Psalm 34:4
Psalm 27:1
II Timothy 1:7
Psalm 87:7 (1-17)
Psalm 118:6,14,17-18
Proverbs 3:21-26
II Chronicles 16:12-13

FREEDOM FROM DOUBT OR UNBELIEF
Psalm 12:1-2
James 1:6-8
Mark 11:22-26
Mark 9:20-27 (especially 24)

WE MUST FORGIVE
> Micah 7:19
> Ezekiel 18:21-22, 30-32
> Mark 11:25-26
> Matthew 6:14-15
> Matthew 18:21-35

GOD'S DESIRE IS LONG LIFE, HEALTH AND HIS PLAN FOR YOUR LIFE
> Psalm 91:16
> Psalm 92:12-15
> Psalm 90:4-12
> Proverbs 3:1-2
> Ephesians 6:1-2
> Exodus 20:12
> Exodus 15:26

PROMISE TO HONOR SEED (CHILDREN) BECAUSE OF THEIR FATHER
> II Kings 10:30
> Leviticus 26:42,44-45a
> Isaiah 44:1-4
> Isaiah 59:16-21 (especially 19,21)

WHY JUDGEMENT OF UNCONFESSED SINS ON SONS OR SEED?
> Exodus 20:5-6
> Ezekiel 24:25
> Psalm 127:5
> Lamentations 5:7 (1-19) (Micah 7:13;
>   Nahum 1:3)
> Daniel 9:11-18
> Deut. 28:15,18
> II Chronicles 34:24-25
> Psalm 106:6
> Psalm 109:13-14
> Job 21:19-20

INIQUITIES OF FATHERS TO BE VISITED ON THEIR SEED (CHILDREN)

Exodus 20:5
Exodus 34:7
Leviticus 16:21,22
Galatians 3:13
II Kings 5:27
Numbers 14:18,33
Acts 3:26
Isaiah 53:11
Romans 4:7
John 9:3
Hebrews 9:12-14
Mark 5:33-34
Deut. 12:23-24
Numbers 14:18
Leviticus 20:4-5
Ezra 9:6-7, 12-15
Ezra 10:1
Joshua 24:20
Job 13:23-26
Job 21:19-20
Psalm 109:4-15 (especially 14)
Isaiah 14:20-22
Isaiah 43:18-28 (especially 21,24,28)
Jeremiah 14:16
Jeremiah 29:32
Jeremiah 32:17-18
Lamentations 5:7
Malachia 2:2-3

EXAMPLES OF INIQUITIES OF FATHERS VISITED ON SONS OR SEED

I Kings 9:6; 11:4,9-11
I Kings 12:28; 14:10; 15:29-30; 13:34
II Kings 9:9
I Kings 16:1-3, 6-7, 11-13
II Kings 9:9, 11-13

EXAMPLES OF INIQUITIES OF FATHERS VISITED ON SONS OR SEED

II Kings 5:27
Job 21:17-20
Jeremiah 36:29-31
II Kings 9:7-10
II Kings 6:32
I Kings 18:4
Numbers 14:33
II Kings 17:14-20
Amalekites Exodus 17:8-16; Numb. 24:20;
    I Samuel 15:33

PATTERNS OF INIQUITIES OF FATHERS SHOWN IN SON'S BEHAVIOR

Amos 2:4
II Kings 14:3
II Kings 14:24
I Kings 18:4
II Peter 2:10-16
Numbers 22:18; 24:13
Psalm 78:1-8
Ezekiel 18:14,17
II Chronicles 26:19-21; 27:1-2
II Chronicles 30:7-9
Jeremiah 11:10
Acts 7:51; 8:23 (14-25)

CONFESSING YOUR INIQUITIES

I John 1:9 (Christian)
Romans 10:9-10,13,4
Ephesians 3:entire (especially 16-21)
Psalm 26:2
Psalm 32:5
Psalm 39:8
Psalm 40:11-13
Psalm 41:8-10
Psalm 65:3-4
Psalm 119:89-94
II Chronicles 7:14-20

CONFESSING YOUR INIQUITIES *Continued*
II Chronicles 34:24-25, 27-28, 31-33
Psalm 51:10-17
Psalm 63:1-5
Psalm 79:8-9
Isaiah 50:1-10 (especially 1,7)
Isaiah 53:4-11
Isaiah 59:2
Isaiah 64:7-9
Jeremiah 31:18-19
Jeremiah 33:3, 6-9a, 11
Jeremiah 36:3
Ezekiel 24:22-23
Ezekiel 28:18
Ezekiel 43:10
Micah 7:18-20
Jeremiah 14:7-9

**CONFESSING THE INIQUITIES OF
YOUR FATHER AND YOURSELF**
Leviticus 26:15-42 (especially 40-41)
Nehemiah 8:18 to 9:3
Nehemiah 13:8 reasoning, praises 12:43
Jeremiah 14:20-22
Psalm 79:8-10
Isaiah 65:6-7 also 8-16
Daniel 9:16-19 (especially 16b)
II Chronicles 29:4-11 (especially 6-9,24)
Hebrews 9:1-28 (especially 14)
II Peter 2:1-22 (especially 14-16)
Isaiah 53:4-11 (especially 6)
Joshua 24:14-24 (especially 15b)
Jeremiah 33:3,11,6-9a
Ezekiel 20:4,30
Micah 7:18-20

SHARING YOUR FREEDOM
Ecclesiastes 5:2-3

SHARING YOUR FREEDOM *Continued*
Psalm 39:1
Proverbs 17:27
Matthew 7:6 (use wisdom)
Proverbs 24:3-7
Isaiah 61:1-3
Matthew 28:18-20
Mark 16:15-20

PRAISES ARE FOR GOD
Hebrews 13:15-16
Matthew 21:15-16
Isaiah 61:3
Psalm 8:2
Job 1: 20-22; 13:15-16
Psalm 18:46
Psalm 20:7
Psalm 21:13
Psalm 22:9-11 and 3
Psalm 26:5-8, 11
Psalm 33:1,18
Psalm 34:1-4
Psalm 35:27-28
Psalm 37:3-5
Psalm 40:3,16
Psalm 46:10
Psalm 47:1
Psalm 50:15,23
Psalm 59:16-17
Psalm 66
Psalm 68:1-4
Psalm 69:30-31
Psalm 71:15-16, 19, 22-24

PRAISES ARE FOR GOD
Psalm 77:14
Psalm 84:4-12
Psalm 89:7-18

PRAISES ARE FOR GOD *Continued*
    Psalm (entire) 91; 96; 97; 98; 99; 100; 111;
        113; 138; 145; 146; 147; 149; 150
    Psalm 104:1-2, 33-35
    Psalm 107:20-22
    Psalm 119:41-50, 62
    II Chronicles 29:27
    Isaiah 43:21
    Isaiah 60:18-19
    (Psalm 91 is read by many families
       at the start of each day.)

ASSURANCE OF GOD'S LOVE AND PROVISION
    Isaiah 44:1-6
    Deut. 6:3-15
    Job 23:8-12
    Job 42:9b-17
    Lamentations 3:25-50
    Psalm 11:17
    Psalm 16:11
    Psalm 18:28-30, 17-18
    Psalm 24:3-5
    Psalm 25:4, 10-12
    Psalm 27:5-6, 14
    Psalm 31:1-5
    Psalm 32:2
    Psalm 34:17-22
    Psalm 37:23-31
    Psalm 60:3-5
    Psalm 61
    Psalm 121
    Psalm 124:8
    Psalm 128:1-6
    Isaiah 54:11-17
    Isaiah 55:2-13
    Proverbs 13:12-15
    Ecclesiastes 2:26
    Nahum 1:7

EXAMPLES OF GOD'S LOVE
Matthew 17:14-18
Luke 8:49-56
Mark 9:17-29
Mark 6:55-56
Luke 7:2-10
Luke 4:33-44
Luke 9:1-6
Luke 10:37-43
Luke 11:1-26
Hebrews 8:10-13
Hebrews 11:6
John 14:12-21 (especially 12-14)
II Peter 5:7

SCRIPTURES TO READ AND MEMORIZE
BEFORE YOU ARE ILL
Psalm 103:3
Psalm 107:20
Proverbs 4:20-22
Isaiah 53:5
Matthew 8:17
I Peter 2:24
Exodus 15:26
Exodus 23:22-25
III John 2
Mark 16:18
Mark 16:15-20
James 5:13-16
Isaiah 54:13-14a, 17
Isaiah 55:11
I Peter 5:7
Hebrews 11:6
John 14:12-14

We are servants of Jehovah God and Jesus. G & M
ETHERIDGE MINISTRIES, INC., Bro. Grady and Myrna
(the author of this work), desire to help and share in your

Christian walk toward "the Mark of the prize of the high calling of God." (Phil. 3:14) Therefore, please write us to let us know how this book affects your life. We especially want to celebrate with you if you have accepted Jesus as Lord and confessed to others that you have.

Our permanent ministry address is:

P.O. Box 564
Sikeston, Missouri 63801
MO (314) 471-9344

PLAN OF SALVATION

Perhaps you do not know Jesus as your personal savior? Here is a prayer for you who want God to indwell your spirit and make you a child of God.

SAMPLE PRAYER

Jesus, I recognize that I am a sinner and need your sacrificial death and blood to cleanse me of my sins.

Please forgive me of my sins and become the Lord of my life. I resign as the lord of my life. I now ask the Holy Spirit to make me a part of the body of Jesus Christ, the true Messiah.

Father God, I thank you that because I confess Jesus and make Him Lord of my life, I am your child. I thank you that I'm forgiven and cleansed of the consequence of my sins. I determine to live as the Bible teaches because I'm now the righteousness of God by the sacrifice of Jesus on the cross. Help me to grow spiritually as I study Your Holy Bible and learn how to live Your way. In Jesus' name, Amen.

WELCOME NEW CREATION!

** Now **

Tell someone what God has done for you.

John 3:16-17
John 1:12-13
Romans 10:9-10
Romans 12:1-3
Romans 6:23
II Timothy 2:15